Complete Conditioning for Pitchers

Sean Cochran

SMC Publishing

Complete Conditioning for Pitchers

Published by
SMC Publishing
12368 Carmel Country Rd. Suite D103
San Diego, CA 92130

For general information on our other products and services or to obtain technical support, please contact us at 858-350-9165 or e-mail support@seancochran.com

Manufactured in the United States of America.

This book is dedicated to Dr. Tom House who was influential in my career and introduction into the sport of baseball.

Contents

Introduction

Increasing velocity, the ability to pitch every fifth day, and how to avoid the "DL" are all questions ask by the MLB pitcher. Today's baseball players in general are stronger, quicker, and more powerful than players even a decade ago. The workloads are high on the pitcher, the number of pitches thrown from the days of little league to the big leagues are greater, and the number of arm injuries appears to have increased dramatically at every level of the game. It is obvious the workloads and stresses on the pitcher are higher today than ever before. As a result the questions begin to arise on how can a pitcher stay healthy, maintain high level workloads, and develop as a pitcher in a successful manner from the high school to the professional ranks.

Even though in this day and age where it is common for ball players to conditioning with weights in the off-season and in-season many questions still arise as to what is the optimal way to condition the body for pitching. Many questions arise such as:

- How do I lift weights and not loose my flexibility?
- What type of weightlifting exercises do I need to perform as a pitcher?
- How often should I train with weights?
- Can I increase my arm speed with strength and conditioning?
- What can I do to avoid arm injuries?

Complete Conditioning for Pitchers answers these questions and many more about what is the proper way to prepare the body for pitching. This book explains and illustrates the proper guidelines, exercises, and programs to follow when developing a pitcher specific strength and conditioning program to allow for optimal performance on the mound. This book will review the needed mobility, flexibility, strength, joint integrity, and endurance required for optimal pitching. The exercises outlined in this book are termed "sports specific" in the strength and conditioning field. Sports specific can be defined as exercises training the body specifically for the physical requirements of a certain sport and position.

Sports specificity for pitchers pertains to the needed energy, muscular, aerobic, and anaerobic requirements for optimal performance in the sport. When we discuss pitchers, we are looking at solving the equation: what exercises and protocols can develop a pitcher for optimal performance and health. *Complete Conditioning for Pitchers* provides the answer to this question and many more.

Unfortunately many players are left in the bull pen when it come to developing their bodies for optimal performance on the mound. As a result, many players are left at a level of performance below their optimum, and others are left injured with a career in doubt. *Complete Conditioning for Pitchers* solves these problems and provides any individual with the proper tools to develop themselves physically for enhanced performance on the mound.

The purpose of this book is to lay out quantified protocols from top to bottom for any individual in baseball. Explanation of the physical requirements of position players in baseball will be discussed. A scientific look at training loads, intensities, and volumes will be laid out for your usage. A discussion of the needed muscular parameters of power, strength, and endurance for baseball will be presented. A discussion of the proper exercises for baseball from flexibility, resistance movements, to agility drills will be presented and mapped out for your benefit. Complete exercise description is given to allow you the proper form and execution of each exercise. A section will provide in-season and off-season conditioning parameters to develop your training program. Overall, this book provides you all the needed information to train efficiently and properly to optimize your performances between the lines.

Chapter One

Biomechanics of Pitching

Biomechanics is the study of human movement. Great strides and increased data based on the biomechanics of pitching have occurred over the past two decades, providing the baseball community with great insight into the kinematics, neuromuscular firing patterns, and physical requirements of pitching.

Leaders in the data capture on the biomechanics of pitching have been Coope Derenne of the University of Hawaii, the American Sports Medicine Institute founded by Dr. James Andrews, and Dr. Tom House currently at the University of Southern California. Through research by these companies and individuals we have learned a vast amount of information about the correlation between the biomechanics of pitching and the human body. We now know how pitchers generate velocity, transfer energy through the body to the release point, and ultimately what is biomechanically necessary to increase throwing velocity and improve arm health.

Pitching Biomechanics

Viewing MLB pitchers we see a variety of arm slots, wind up characteristics, release points, and follow through. Regardless of these "style" differentiations, commonalities exist within all of these pitchers providing for a successful "pitch" at the highest level of competition.

The goal of this book is to provide the pitcher a resource to condition the body to successfully execute the throwing motion. That being said, it is imperative we have a base understanding of the mechanics associated with the pitching motion. This will provide us a conceptual understanding of why we are implementing certain training modalities and why an exercise is conducive to the pitching motion.

The pitching motion is generally classified as an overhead throwing motion. The focus of many studies center upon the shoulder's complex involvement in the throwing motion. We recognize the pitching motion is a total body activity beginning with lower extremities, moving up through the kinetic chain into the pelvis, torso, and advancing to the shoulder, elbow, wrist, and hand at release point.

Research indicates deviation from this aforementioned segmental activity can affect outcome of the pitch in terms of velocity, accuracy, and stresses placed upon the kinetic chain.

Phases of the Pitching Motion

Pitching coaches, researchers on the biomechanics of pitching, and coaches in general will define the phases of pitching differently in terms of the number of phases, what occurs in each phase, and how to develop the pitcher in general. To establish a baseline for this book we will provide the reader a basic synopsis of the phases of pitching for reference purposes. The pitching motion in the most basic of terms has four phases; (1) Windup, (2) Cocking, (3) Acceleration and (4) Follow Through.

Windup

The windup is considered the setting phase of the pitching motion. The goal of the windup is to set the kinetic chain in motion in the correct sequence and timing. The windup begins at a set position with the glove hand and ball hand together. The contra lateral leg begins the motion within the pitching action and the ipsilateral leg is the support or balance leg. (Dillman, Fleisig, & Andrews, 1993) A weight transfer will occur during the windup with a body rotation of up to 90-120 degrees. The windup is a considered a preparation phase where the body is loading the kinetic chain in preparation for the cocking phase.

Cocking

The cocking phase is the second phase of the pitching motion. Most models indicate the cocking phase begins when the hands separate and is complete when the throwing shoulder is completely abducted and laterally rotated. (Pappas et. Al., 1985) The majority of pitching models separate the cocking phase into an early and late phase. The early cocking phase is categorized with activity surrounding the arm movement and scapula retraction. The late cocking phase begins with the stride foot coming into contact with the ground (Jobe et, al. 1984) The late cocking phase will encapsulate both arms elevated and in-line with the shoulders. Research indicates stress on the anterior potion of the gleno-humeral joint is high at this position within the throwing motion. The deltoid is extremely active in this phase and stabilizers of the upper torso and shoulder are predominant to restrain the throwing motion. Further research indicates the scapula stabilizers are active and reciprocal inhibition occurs in the rotator cuff to resist the subluxation forces in the torso from the forward lean. (Jobe et al. 1984)

At the end portion of this phase the shoulder complex medial rotators are maximally stretched, the pelvis is leading the shoulder to facing home plate, (Braatz & Gogia, 1987) shoulder rotation to home plate, and lateral trunk activity are facilitated by the non-throwing arm's motion. (House, 1995)

Acceleration

According to House acceleration begins with maximum lateral rotation of the shoulder and is complete when the ball is released from the pitcher's hand. Scapular protraction, humeral head horizontal flexion, medial rotation of the humeral head, and elbow extension occur in this phase. (Jobe, et al, 1984) During the acceleration phase arm speed has increased significantly in a very short time. Research indicates a maximum speed of 7500 degrees per second are reached by the end of this phase. (Pappas et al, 1985)

Follow Through

The follow through phase of the pitching motion occurs after the ball is released to home plate. This phase entails the slowing down of the kinetic chain and dissipation of energy not directed into the baseball. Deceleration of the arm occurs during the follow through and entails high levels of activity from the deltoid, biceps, and rotator cuff. (Braatz & Gogia, 1987) Research indicates a high number of posterior shoulder injuries occurring in this phase due to the required dissipation of energy. (House, 1992)

Summary

Providing a basic synopsis on the biomechanics of pitching and phases of the throwing motion provides us the base information on how to develop the body around the requirements of the pitcher. We recognize how the kinetic chain is integral in the generation of arm speed, the stress placed upon the body, and what is necessary in terms of a strength and conditioning programs for the pitcher. It is invariably understood from this information physical parameters must be present in the kinetic chain in order to execute a proficient pitching motion which generates maximum arm speed and prevents injury. The next chapter will build on this information and decipher what is required on the "physical side" of this equation.

Chapter Two

Guidelines to Training the Pitcher

Now that you have a basic understanding of the Biomechanics of pitching let's delve further into the physical requirements of pitching. We must remind ourselves pitching involves the generation of speed through the body which is released into the baseball. In order to execute this athletic action efficiently with the least amount of stress on the arm, the body must have a sound physical foundation. This physical foundation is rooted in the concepts of flexibility, mobility, stability, strength, and power.

That being said, we must recognize the importance of developing all these base physical components involved in executing the pitching motion. The process where the development of the pitcher or any athlete begins is what I term the "five physical pillars" of sport. They are: Mobility, neuromuscular efficiency, stability, endurance, and power. The cohesive combination of these physical parameters creates the foundation for the execution of the athletic actions associated with pitching

To improve performance, increase arm speed, maintain arm health, and prevent injury, it is necessary to develop the "five physical pillars" of the kinetic chain. Empirical evidence also suggests it is best to develop these physical components in order. Begin with mobility, then progressing to neuromuscular efficiency, and completing the process with power training. Following this sequence provides the correct ratios of mobility to stability, and prevents the possibility of injury to a player who is not physically ready to implement a specific training modality.

The goal of your strength and conditioning program as a pitcher is to develop a physical foundation allowing you to execute the athletic actions associated with pitching efficiently and effectively. This is accomplished through the development of the "five physical pillars" of your body. We will now look at what is required from your body in terms of mobility, neuromuscular efficiency, stability, endurance, and power. Exercises correlating to these categories and programs will be discussed in future chapters.

Mobility/Stability Pattern

Before breaking down the "five physical pillars" of pitching individually it is important to discuss a concept very central to athletic development. The concept we are referring to is the mobility/stability pattern of human movement. This principle was first noted by physical therapist Gray Cook and strength coach Mike Boyle. This principle states efficient movement within the kinetic chain of the human body occurs in an alternating pattern of mobile joints and stable segments. If this pattern of mobile joints and stable segments is altered, dysfunction in movement patterns will occur, and compensations in these movement patterns will be the result. Table 1.2 below provides a joint-by-joint view of this pattern within the human body.

Table 1.2 Mobility/Stability Pattern

Foot	Stable
Ankle	Mobile
Knee	Stable
Hip	Mobile
Pelvis/Sacral/Lumbar Spine	Stable
Thoracic Spine	Mobile
Scapula-Thoracic	Stable
Gleno-Humeral/Shoulder	Mobile
Elbow	Stable
Wrist	Mobile
Cervical Spine	Stable

As you can see from the above table the human body "feet to fingertips" operates in an alternating pattern of a mobile joint followed by a stable joint throughout the entire kinetic chain (i.e. body). It is obvious joints such as the elbow and knee are not rod like pieces of iron that do not flex or extend, but rather these joints are stable in terms of limited degrees of motion. For example, the knee joint does not rotate in 360 degrees of motion as does the hip or shoulder, rather it operates essentially in one plane of motion flexing and extending. As a result this joint is considered a stable joint where as the hip, shoulder, and ankle require large ranges of motion for human movement to occur efficiently.

Relative to pitching the mobility/stability pattern of human movement allows for the creation and transfer of energy through the kinetic chain from "feet to fingertips" into the baseball at your release point. If the mobility/ stability pattern is dysfunctional relative to the pitching motion, the development of speed will be limited, transfers of this speed to the ball will be compromised, and the ability to execute a repeatable throwing motion will most likely be limited.

For example, if a pitcher had limited hip mobility. The ability to rotate the hips after foot strike on the mound would be limited, and the transfer of speed could be hindered in addition to greater stresses placed upon other parts of the body. This would result in a loss of speed, an inefficient transfer of this speed to the ball, and most likely the development of compensations in the pitching motion.

As you can see from the above example, the mobility/stability pattern of human movement is integral to pitching and deficiencies within it will adversely affect every aspect of the pitcher from velocity, accuracy, and arm health. Development of the "five physical pillars" supports the mobility/stability pattern of human movement and are a great benefit to it.

Mobility

The first pillar is mobility. Mobility is a combination of both joint range of motion and flexibility. Joint range of motion concerns itself with the actual articular structure of the joint (i.e. skeletal structures), and flexibility has to do with the extensibility of the soft tissues (muscles, tendons, ligaments) surrounding the joint. To better understand the relationship of joint range of motion and flexibility let's define both.

Flexibility can be defined as the optimal extensibility of all soft tissues surrounding a joint to allow for full range of motion. (Michael Clark, Director: National Academy of Sports Medicine) If certain muscles are "tight" or ligaments become "un-pliable" the ability for a joint to move through multiple ranges of motion may be hindered. For example, pitching requires the hip to be mobile in order to execute correctly. If the surrounding soft tissues (ligaments, muscles, tendons) are "tight" the hip will be immobile and unable to operate through the ranges of motion required too execute the rotation of the hips after foot strike in the pitching motion.

In addition to flexibility, range of motion is the second component of mobility. Mobility as stated above is the combination of normal joint range of motion and proper extensibility of the surrounding soft tissues. Range of motion is simply the number of degrees a joint should be able to flex, extend, or rotate. For example, the elbow joint is considered a hinge joint that only flexes and extends. The elbow joint should flex or extend a certain number of degrees. Limitations in the degrees of flexion and extension would be considered a limited range of motion in relation to the elbow joint.

Mobility could be limited by a lack of extensibility by the surrounding soft tissues of a joint or the articular (i.e. skeletal) structures of the joint. For example, if the ankle joint were to have bone spurs, mobility in this joint would be limited not from the soft tissues surrounding the joint, but rather the articular components of the joint. Typically, mobility issues for baseball players are a result of flexibility issues rather than joint range of motion.

Neuromuscular Efficiency

The second "physical pillar" is neuromuscular efficiency, which is often referred to as balance. It is defined as the ability of the neuromuscular system (nervous and muscular systems) to maintain the proper alignment, center of gravity, and coordinate the body during biomechanical movement. (Gray Cook, Athletic Body in Balance, 34) Throughout the entire pitching motion, it is necessary for the ball player to maintain certain angles, create a weight transfer, coordinate muscular movements, and generate speed. To perform this properly, you must be able to maintain balance of the body as a unit and control your extremities (i.e. arms and legs).

Neuromuscular efficiency within baseball is a responsibility of both the body and the mechanics by which you pitch. Improvement of your neuromuscular efficiency capacities on the "physical side of the equation" will allow your body to execute the athletic actions associated with baseball with greater efficiency and ease.

The process by which the athlete improves their neuromuscular efficiency is via specified exercises challenging the body's current state of balance, movement coordination, and kinesthetic awareness. Over time these training modalities will improve one's neuromuscular efficiency and overall athleticism.

Stability

Stability is the third pillar of our five pillars. Stability can be defined as the ability of any system to remain unchanged or aligned in the presence of outside forces (Greg Rose, Titleist Performance Institute Manual, 86) The development of stability within the neuromuscular system is contingent upon muscular strength. Strength is defined as the ability of your body to exert the required levels of force to perform the functional movement at hand. (Michael Clark, Integrated Training for the New Millennium, 369)

Basically, stability in the pitching is contingent upon muscular strength, and in order to execute the pitching motion effectively and generate velocity, a certain level of muscular strength is required. This allows your body to correctly sequence the muscular contractions required in pitching, maintain the postural positions associated with the motion, and provide a base for arm health.

Stability tends to be the "stumbling block" for many younger ball players. They simply do not have the muscular strength in their bodies to execute the pitching motion efficiently over an extended period of time. The result is sometimes what we refer to as an "arm thrower", or an individual whose velocity decreases as the pitch count increases, or it "shows up" in an inability to hit their spots due to arm fatigue.

Endurance

The fourth pillar of your strength and conditioning program for pitching is muscular endurance. Muscular endurance is the ability of a muscle(s) to repeatedly perform a physical action over an extended period of time without fatigue. Performing repeated physical actions such as the pitching motion causes fatigue within the muscular system. As a result, muscular performance can decrease. Once this occurs the ability to pitch will decrease and potential for injury increases. Endurance as with muscular strength is again a problem area for many younger players and older players when the season becomes longer and more games are played. As is the case with muscular strength, the ball player does not have the endurance capacities developed within their neuromuscular systems required for pitching. Over time the result is a decrease in performance, increased stresses on the body, and a much higher potential for injury. To prevent such a situation from occurring during a game or season, it is necessary to develop muscular endurance.

Power

Muscular power is the final physical pillar and final factor necessary for optimal performance on the mound.

Muscular power can be defined as the ability of the body to create the greatest amount of force in a short amount of time. (Vladimir Zatsiorsky, Professor Department of Exercise and Sport Science, Pennsylvania State University) Basically, power is one component of developing arm speed. The more speed that can be developed by the body the more potential for increases in arm speed. So it is a great attribute for any pitcher, junior player included, to develop the power components of the body.

We often do not associated power training as an integral component of the pitcher as the pitching motion utilizes a kinetic energy chain to gradually increase speed through the body into release point. Even though this is the case increasing the power outputs of the body will only benefit this speed generation in the pitching motion.

In order to increase the power outputs of your muscles, it is necessary to implement specialized exercises. These types of exercises, referred to as plyometrics, jump training, Olympic lifting, or med ball work will enhance the ability of your neuromuscular system to develop power, which in turn, as stated above, will enhance the amount of speed generated by the body. Typically for pitchers, plyometrics and med ball work are utilized for power development as the Olympic lifts for overhead throwing athletes have a high risk-reward ratio to benefit the pitcher.

Summary

Let's put all this information together so you have a solid understanding before moving on. Mobility, neuromuscular efficiency, stability, endurance, and power comprise the "five physical pillars" of the athlete. The "five physical pillars" of the athlete support the mobility/stability pattern of human movement. Development of these five pillars is necessary to execute the biomechanics of pitching correctly. Inefficiencies in any one or all five of these categories will directly affect the execution of throwing the baseball. The athlete will often have physical deficiencies within the areas of neuromuscular efficiency, stability, endurance, and power development hindering the ability to perform optimally and maintain health as a pitcher.

Chapter Three

Strength & Conditioning Principles

In order to develop the "five physical pillars" of the pitcher athlete in a strength and conditioning program, it is necessary for you to adhere to certain training principles. These training principles will assist in developing a systematic approach in the development of the neuromuscular system relative to the pitching The training principles we will discuss in this chapter are cross-specificity, adaptation, overload, progression, functional, and periodization.

Cross-specificity

Cross-specificity is a reference to the similarities between a training program, exercises, and modalities relative to your chosen sport. In order to develop your body around the requirements of pitching; you must choose exercises simulating the biomechanics of the pitching motion, utilize training modalities developing the mobility/ stability pattern of human movement, and train the kinetic chain to the requirements of the pitching motion.

For example, during the throwing motion, rotation occurs in the core section of the body during stride to home plate. In order for your body to execute this requirement of the pitching motion more effectively and efficiently, you need to develop mobility in the hips and stability in the lumbar spine. Such a task can be accomplished through cross-specific training defined as the training of the body to the anatomical positions, movements, and physical requirements of the athlete's chosen sport. (Carlos Santana, Director, Institute of Human Performance) This type of program is the foundation for the development of mobility, balance, stability, endurance, and power around pitching.

The implementation of a cross-specific training program creates a transfer-of-training effect into your throwing motion. A transfer-of-training effect is the ability of a training program to have a direct benefit on the performance of the athlete during competition. (Juan Carlos Santana, Institute of Performance, Boca Raton, FL) To better understand this concept let us use the example of a marathon runner and interior lineman in American football. The marathon runner and lineman are required to train extensively to perform in demanding environments. Both athletes spend many hours training for the rigors of either a marathon or professional football season. Now, consider what would happen if each were to trade training programs. Both athletes in all likelihood would perform poorly in their chosen sport. Why is this case? The demands placed upon the body by each of these sports are different and thus requires a strength and conditioning program specific to the physical needs of the sport. Baseball and pitching is no different and for this reason it is imperative to utilize the principle of cross-specificity.

Adaptation

The ability of the body to adapt to the demands placed upon it by external stimuli is the principle of adaptation. All forms of strength training are based upon this principle. For your body to improve its strength, neuromuscular efficiency, endurance, power, or flexibility, an external stimuli beyond your normal activity levels must be provided. For example, when you continue to perform flexibility exercises for the hips or stability exercises for the core, your body will adapt by becoming more flexible and strong. Another example would be increasing the strength and endurance capacities of the shoulder complex to benefit the pitcher with less arm fatigue. To develop the physical pillars required of pitching you must provide a stimulus in the form of exercise to create the necessary adaptation.

Overload

The overload principle states the human body will adapt to the increased resistance placed upon it by becoming stronger, faster, or more flexible. To improve your flexibility, balance, strength, endurance, or power you need to continually stress your body beyond what it has experienced in the past. For example, to constantly improve the strength within your lower body, increasing the load (weight) of your lower body resistance training exercises would create an overload on the body. Over time this increase in load would result in a stronger lower body.

Relative to resistance training and overload, it is often thought the only way to overload the neuromuscular systems is through the utilization of dumbbells and barbells (i.e. weight training). This is untrue as many modalities can be utilized and the process by which the baseball player will overload the neuromuscular system will be covered in later chapters.

Remember, for any physical improvement it is necessary to place an overload on your muscular system, and that overload may take the form of many different methods of training outside of dumbbells and barbells. The next principle, progression describes how to utilize the overload principle in relation to the principle of adaptation.

Progression

Progression is the implementation of exercises that progressively force the muscular and nervous systems of the body to work harder. In turn, this places an overload on these systems forcing the body to adapt over time. For example, if you started to perform a standard bicep curl with 25 lb. dumbbells for 15 repetitions, the exercise would be difficult at first. The reason for the difficulty is the curling action with 25 lbs. is above and beyond what your muscles are accustomed too (i.e. overload). Over time your body would adapt to the 25 lb. dumbbells (principle of adaptation) and if your desire was to continue to get stronger biceps, it would be necessary to progress (principle of progression) to a more challenging weight or exercise.

This is a simple example of the principle of progression at work. Progressions for cross-specific exercise for pitchers follow some simple guidelines: begin with static exercises (stationary) and progress to dynamic (moving); begin with slow exercise movements and advance to fast; start with exercises in a stable environment and move to an unstable training environment, progress from bilateral extremity exercises to unilateral; commence with low force output exercises and progress to high output.

A sample progression for a high school level pitcher implementing resistance training for the lower body could be as follows:

1. Stationary two-legged body weight squat – progression number one: body weight split squat – progression number two: body weight single leg squat

2. Good mornings – progression number one: two-legged medicine ball dead lift – progression number two: single leg medicine ball dead lift

This is a simple progression of both lower body hip and knee dominant exercises, and as you can see the exercises progressively overload the neuromuscular system as the body adapts.

Functional

Functional is a word that is almost overused in the field of strength and conditioning in this day and age, but it still has a great amount of importance relative to performance training for a sport. Functional can be defined as the development of physical components of the body with the intent on improving the athlete within their chosen sport. Baseball and pitching is no different. Training the baseball player athlete should utilize functional training modalities improving the mobility, stability, strength, and endurance of the athlete for competition on the diamond. We are not concerned about the size of their biceps or triceps. A tough sell at times for the younger player, as often a desire exists for aesthetics. The type of training which gives you those "beach muscles" will not necessarily improve arm speed or improve arm health.

Functional training modalities are characterized by exercises training the body in multiple planes of motion, requiring the muscles of the body to accelerate and decelerate movements in multiple planes of motion, and force the kinetic chain (i.e. body) to stabilize during these movement patterns.

Periodization

Most athletes use what is called a periodization schedule to plan their training. Periodizaton is the cycling of loads, volumes, intensity, and exercises within a given time period. The time frame may be divided into days, weeks, months, or even years. The cycling allows for a systematic approach to achieving improvement in your flexibility, balance, strength, endurance, and power as well as prevents overtraining.

Professional baseball typically utilize a periodization program splitting the year into three separate time frames; off-season, in-season, and pre-season. The off-season for the professional player will focus on developing increased levels of flexibility, balance, strength, endurance, and power for the upcoming season. The pre-season portion of the program will typically reduce the amount of physical training performed by the athlete to allow them the energy required for the increased practice time and bull pen sessions in spring training. Lastly, the in-season portion will focus on keeping the player injury free and on the mound. The greatest difference between all three segments is the amount of work (i.e. volume) performed. Off-season programs are high volume, pre-season are moderate volume, and in-season programs are low volume workouts.

The high school or collegiate level player can utilize a periodization program similar to the professional baseball. Pitchers at these levels can split the year into definitive off-season, pre-season, and in-season training periods. Sample periodization programs for the high school and collegiate player can be found in the latter chapters of this book.

Intensity, Load, Volume, Duration, Frequency

Intensity is the amount of work for a specific exercise, groups of exercises, or entire training program. Different intensity levels of training will cause differing adaptations within your neuromuscular system. For example, if you were to perform lunges using a repetition range of 15-20 per set with 20 lb. dumbbells, this would elicit an increase in the muscular endurance capacities of your lower body. If the decision was then made to increase the strength capacities of your lower body using this exercise, changes in the amount of weight and repetitions would be needed. You might decide to use 40 lb. dumbbells allowing you to complete 6 repetitions of this exercise. This would shift the adaptation of the muscles in your lower body from increased endurance to increased strength levels.

The four variables- load, volume, duration, and frequency can be modified as a group or individually to increase the intensity of your training program. Let's take a close look at these variables for a better understanding.

Volume is the total amount of work performed in a given exercise, exercises, or entire workout. It is usually equated by multiplying the load x repetitions. For example, a dumbbell lunge performed with 60 lb. dumbbells for 12 repetitions would equate to a training volume of 720 lbs. for the exercise.

Load refers to the amount of resistance utilized for a given exercise. Load can be equated in the form of body weight, elastic resistance, or in the form of external resistance such as weight vests, medicine balls, dumbbells, or barbells. Repetitions and load are often linked. High repetition exercises typically require lighter loads, whereas low repetition exercises utilize heavier loads.

Duration is the amount of time between each exercise within a specific workout. This training variable is often confused with frequency. Duration is strictly the rest period between sets. Typically a decrease in rest periods between sets increases the intensity of the workout. For example, a decrease in the rest periods between two sets of body weight squats from 60 seconds down to 30 seconds would increase the intensity of the exercises simply because the body is not resting as much between sets.

Frequency is the number of training sessions in a specified time period. An increase in the number of training sessions within a set time period elicits a higher training intensity for the overall program. For example, increasing the number of workouts to four from three in a seven-day time frame increases the overall intensity of the training program.

Always remember this: the intensity levels of your training elicit different adaptations within your neuromuscular system. A few examples should give you a very good understanding of this concept. A pitchers who needs increased muscular strength in their legs would use a moderate load, repetition range, and volume to achieve the training intensity to elicit such results. Another pitcher interested in increasing the endurance levels of their lower body would use lighter loads, higher repetition ranges, and volumes to achieve the training intensity and desired result. See the table below for detailed information on training intensity and variables for a better understanding.

Table 1.3   Training Intensity and Training Variables

TRAINING TYPE	LOAD/INTENSITY	REPETITION	DURATION/FREQUENCY
STRENGTH	70-90%	6-12 PER SET	1-2 min. 3-4 TIMES PER WEEK
ENDURANCE	70% <	15-25 PER SET	30 s. 3-4 TIMES PER WEEK
POWER	90%>	8 < PER SET	2-3 min. 2-4 TIMES PER WEEK

Before moving on, it is necessary you understand how each training variable affects intensity levels and adaptations by your body. For a full understanding review the table above and the information in the previous chapter on muscular strength, endurance, and power.

Summary

Let's put it all together so you feel comfortable before moving on. The training principles of cross-specificity, adaptation, overload, progression, functional, and periodization directly influence your training program. To improve your play on the field, match up the mechanics of the pitching motion and athletic requirements of baseball to the exercises in your training program (cross-specificity training). This allows for a transfer of training effect to occur within your game. Exercises that are functional are best for the athlete. The body adapts to stresses placed upon it, so for continual improvement the body requires overload of the neuromuscular system. It is best to utilize a systematic approach (progression) to achieve this goal.

Intensity is the amount of work performed in a given exercise, group of exercises, or entire workout. The intensity level of your training directly affects the adaptations by your body in the areas of muscular strength, endurance, and power. The training variables of load, volume, duration, and frequency directly affect the training intensity of your workout. These variables can be altered individually or as a group to elicit different outcomes from your workouts. Remember to be specific in terms of your training intensity to achieve the desired adaptations in your body.

Baseball players of all ages must pay strict attention to these training principles. Adherence to these principles will allow you to develop the physical parameters of the body for the sport of baseball and requirements of pitching.

That being said, how resistance training is implemented to increase training intensity is very important for the athlete. Empirical evidence suggests it is best for the athletes with little training experience to begin with exercises that are body weight orientated in terms of resistance, and progress to externally loading the body in the form of weighted vests, elastic tubing, medicine balls, barbells, and dumbbells. All too often younger players will implement heavy loads in the form of barbells and dumbbells when the kinetic chain (i.e. body) is not ready for such loads.

Chapter Four

Baseball Assessment

The assessments listed below are geared towards measuring an individual's flexibility, mobility, balance, stability, strength, and power relative to the requirements of pitching. The information gathered from these assessments will help determine the strengths and weaknesses of your physical makeup relative to athletic movement patterns. Not only will these assessments provide relative information for the improvement of your pitching motion, they also function as a tool for the development of your strength and conditioning program, the setting of goals, and measuring results.

Fitness Assessment

The physical assessments in this chapter will provide you an abundance of information on where in the kinetic chain limitations affecting athletic actions are present. These assessments cover the categories of posture, flexibility, mobility, neuromuscular efficiency, muscular strength, endurance, and power. Guidelines for the tests are provided and I strongly suggest you re-test yourself every 6-8 weeks to track your progress.

To ensure safety and reliability, each assessment should be performed with strict attention to proper execution. Follow the instructions for each of the tests and record your results. To provide you with the most accurate results, I recommend performing the tests in the order they are written.

Very little equipment is needed to complete these tests. I recommend you make use of a stopwatch, medicine ball (3-6 lbs.), and tape measure. Remember these tests in addition to determining the "weak links" in your kinetic chain, help you determine where to start your training programs, what areas to focus on in your conditioning program, and ultimately, the goals of your strength training program. Keeping a journal of all your tests results is also recommended. A journal allows you to review your tests to chart progress and set new goals. Now let's move onto the actual tests.

Assessment Procedures

Listed below are a series of tests to provide you with information on your posture, levels of flexibility, mobility, neuromuscular efficiency, strength, endurance, and power. Before performing any of these tests, be sure to be in good health and cleared by your personal physician. If you are uncomfortable or feel physically unable to perform a certain test, feel free to move onto the next one. For accuracy, perform each assessment 2-3 times, and in the order they are presented.

Postural Assessment

Poor posture leads to muscular imbalances, chronic injury, and less than optimal athletic outputs. It is of great importance to determine if postural deficiencies exist within your body. This will allow you to address this situation with the correct flexibility, mobility, balance, and strength training exercises. Listed below is a postural assessment to determine any mobility and stability limitations joint-by-joint in the body, beginning with the ankle, and progressing up the kinetic chain.

In addition to indicating any structural deficiencies, the static postural assessment will also provide insight into any muscular imbalances within the body. Often times players due to the unilateral activities within baseball will suffer from muscle imbalances where over development in one area of the body is causing dysfunction in another.

To perform this assessment correctly you will need a full-length mirror. Using an erasable marker or piece of tape, mark a vertical line directly in the middle of the mirror. Make sure the line covers the full length of the mirror and is straight.

Stand comfortably in front of the mirror at a distance where you can view your entire body. Align your body in the center of the mirror allowing the line on the mirror to dissect the middle of your body. Stand with feet slightly closer than shoulder width, hands resting at your sides, and eyes looking directly forward. This is the starting position of your static postural assessment.

The postural assessment will entail a visual observation of each joint in your body beginning with the ankle and working up the skeletal system to the shoulders. Each joint in your body, when viewed in the mirror, should be aligned straight with the mirror. For example the kneecap should point directly towards the mirror (internal or external rotation of the knee indicates a postural deficiency). In addition to joint alignment, observe each joint in relation to its opposing joint. For example, the right and left shoulders should be horizontally aligned. If the right shoulder is higher than the left this again is an indicator of muscular imbalances and joint restriction.

Listed in the table below are the visual cues to observe in each joint as you progress through the static postural assessment. Pay strict attention to each joint, stay relaxed, and utilize the information from this assessment to develop your golf fitness program.

Ankle	Internal Rotation (yes)	Tight Muscles – Adductors
		Weak Muscles – IT Band, Glute
		Medius, Glute Maximus
	Suggested Exercises	90/90 Hamstring, Bent Knee Back Hold

Ankle	External Rotation (yes)	Tight Muscles – IT Band, Glute Medius, Glute Maximus
	Suggested Exercises	Seated Hamstring Stretch w/ PB, Hip Circles
Knee	Internal Rotation (yes)	Tight Muscles – Adductors, Piriformis
		Weak Muscles - Glute Medius, Glute Maximus
	Suggested Exercises	90/90 Hamstring Stretch, Tubing Walks
Knee	External Rotation (yes)	Tight Muscles – IT Band, Glute Medius, Glute Maximus
		Weak Muscles – Adductors
	Suggested Exercises	Side Leg Raise - Adduction
Hip	Increased Extension (yes)	Tight Muscles – Erector Spinae
		Weak Muscles – Psoas, Abdominals
	Suggested Exercises	Cats Down, Cats Up, Crunch, Reverse Crunch
Hip	Increased Flexion (yes)	Tight Muscles - Rectus Abdominis
		Weak Muscles - Erector Spinae
	Suggested Exercises	Back Flexion w/ PB, Alternating Arm & Leg Extension
Shoulders	Internal Rotation (yes)	Tight Muscles - Pectoralis Major, Subscapularis
		Weak Muscles - Trapezius, Rhomboid
	Suggested Exercises	Chest Stretch w/ PB, Dumbbell Row
Shoulders	External Rotation (yes)	Tight Muscles – Trapezius, Latimus Dorsi
		Weak Muscles - Pectoralis Major
	Suggested Exercises	Lat Stretch w/ PB, Push Up

Flexibility/Mobility Assessment

A lack of flexibility or mobility creates joint restrictions and the inability to move the body through the required ranges of motion of the throwing motion. The utilization of flexibility and mobility assessments can assist in pinpointing muscles or joints that may be restricting your throwing motion and causing compensations. Listed below are a series of flexibility and mobility assessments to assist in this process. Pay strict attention to technique when performing these assessments and record your results.

Anterior Shoulder Test

Procedure

Lay flat on your back on the floor, knees bent, and hands resting at your sides.

Place hands behind your head and clasp fingers together.

Allow arms and elbows to relax.

Normal flexibility is when both elbows rest comfortably on the floor and tightness is not felt in the anterior shoulder.

Standing Rotation Test

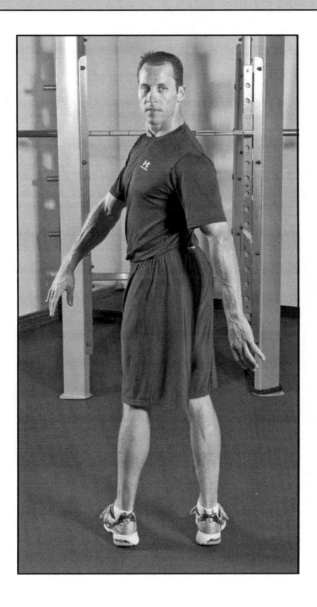

Procedure

Stand upright, feet slightly close than shoulder width, toes pointed forward, arms resting at sides, and back facing a mirror.

Keeping the feet in place slowly rotate to the right allowing the hips, torso, and shoulders to turn.

Rotate as far as possible allowing your head to face the mirror. Pause and obverse your hips and shoulders.

Normal rotation flexibility is when the hips are rotated approximately 45 degrees and the shoulders 90 degrees without discomfort or pain.

Repeat the rotation test to your left and again observe the amount of rotation in the hips and shoulders.

Back Scratch Test

Procedure

Stand upright, hands on your hips, and eyes looking forward.

Reach over your right shoulder with the right arm.

Simultaneously reach behind your back with the left arm.

Attempt to touch the right and left thumbs together.

Repeat the test reaching the left arm over the left shoulder, and the right arm behind your back.

Normal flexibility of the shoulder capsule is when a "gap" of 4 inches or less exists between the thumbs in either position.

Overhead Reach Test

Procedure

Stand upright with back flat on a wall, hands on your hips, and eyes looking forward.

Simultaneously elevate both arms overhead, attempting to touch the wall with both thumbs.

Normal upper and mid-back flexibility is when the thumbs can touch the wall with the upper and mid-back maintaining contact with the wall.

Standing Toe Touch Test

Procedure

Stand upright with feet together, torso upright, eyes looking forward, arms overhead, and fingers together.

Slowly bend at the hips and lower the hands with the arms straight towards your toes.

Continue to bend forward at the hips keeping the knees straight.

Reach downward with the hands as far as possible trying to touch your fingers to the toes.

Normal flexibility is when the fingertips can touch the toes without the knees bending or discomfort in the lower back.

Cats Down and Up Test

Procedure

Place both of your hands on the floor directly under the shoulders.

Position both of your knees directly under the hips, eyes looking down and back flat.

Begin by rounding the lower back down towards the floor, simultaneously extending your head upward, keep the arms straight throughout the entire movement.

Continue by extending your lower back upward towards the ceiling, arch the lower back up until it is rounded. Keep the arms straight throughout the movement.

Normal lower back mobility is when the back can fully round upward and arch downward without any feelings of tightness or restriction.

Prayer Position Reach Test

Procedure

Position both hands on the floor directly under the shoulders. Position both of your knees directly under the hips, eyes looking down and back flat.

Pull the hips backward towards the heels keeping the hands in place. Continue to pull the hips backward until the glutes are resting on your heels.

Rotate the palm of the left hand upward and attempt to elevate the hand off the floor while keeping the arm straight. Repeat the test with the right hand.

Normal mobility in the shoulder is when the hand can be elevated off the floor while the arm is straight and body remains in the "prayer position".

Neuromuscular Efficiency

An assessment of your neuromuscular efficiency will indicate inefficiencies in the coordination of movement and any core or kinetic chain stability issues. It is best to perform these assessments in front of a mirror. This will allow you to observe the execution of each assessment. Progress through the assessment exercises listed below at a comfortable pace, and take notes on any difficulties within each assessment.

Seated Leg Extension Test

Procedure

Sit upright on a physio-ball, hands on your hips, torso upright, and eyes looking forward.

Place your feet shoulder width apart, feet planted firmly on the floor, and knees bent at 90 degrees.

Slowly extend the lower leg straight, maintaining your upright posture on the ball.

Attempt to extend the left leg to a straight position and hold for one second, repeat with the right leg.

Perform a total of 10 repetitions of the assessment.

On a scale of 1 to 10 (10 being the most difficult) determine the level of difficulty in the performance of this assessment and record your results. A score of 1-3 is excellent, 3-5 average, above 5 below average.

Single Leg Balance Test

Procedure

Stand upright in front of a mirror, feet slightly closer than shoulder width, hands on your hips, torso upright, and eyes looking forward.

Begin by lifting the left foot one off the floor, left knee inline with hip, and attempt to balance on the right leg.

Attempt to keep the hands on your hips and torso upright. Record the amount of time you are able to balance on the right foot. Repeat this assessment by balancing on your left foot again recording your time.

In addition, on a scale of 1 to 10 (10 being the most difficult) determine the level of difficulty in the performance of this assessment and record your results.

An ability to maintain balance for over 45 seconds is excellent, 30-45 seconds good, 15-30 average, less than 15 seconds below average.

Single Leg Toe Touch Test

Procedure

Stand upright in front of a mirror, feet slightly close than shoulder width, right hand on your hip, and left arm extended over head.

Begin by lifting the left foot off the floor and balancing on the right leg.

Proceed with this assessment by reaching the left hand down towards the right foot by hinging at the hip and keeping the right leg straight. Do not permit the left foot to touch the floor during the movement, and continue to reach the right hand towards the top of the left foot.

Return to the starting position and attempt to perform 10 repetitions of this assessment. Once complete repeat the assessment balancing on the left leg and reaching with the right arm.

Once complete on a scale of 1 to 10 (10 being the most difficult) determine the level of difficulty on the performance of this assessment and record your results. Pay attention to the ability to hinge at the hip while performing this assessment. A score of 1-3 is excellent, 3-5 good, above 5 less than average.

Stability Assessment

In order to generate arm speed, create a repeatable delivery, and execute all athletic actions proficiently, certain segments of the body must be stable. Recalling from previous chapters, an integral component of stability is muscular strength. The assessments listed below will measure strength land endurance levels relative to baseball and the throwing motion. Pay strict attention to technique during the execution of these assessments.

Stationary Squat Test

A stopwatch will be required for this test.

Procedure

Begin by placing your feet shoulder width apart and arms extended straight.

Slowly squat downward to a position where your knees are bent at 90 degrees.

Maintain this position and time yourself.

Record the amount of time you can "hold" the correct position of the test. A time of over 2 minutes is excellent, 90 seconds good, 60 seconds fair, less than 60 seconds poor.

Bent Knee Back Hold Test

Use a stopwatch to time yourself.

Procedure

Lay with your back flat on the floor, knees bent, and feet together.

Elevate your hips off the floor inline with your knees and shoulders.

Do not arch the lower back or allow the hips to sag. Squeeze your glutes and hold this position.

Record the amount of time you can "hold" the correct position of the test.

A time of over 2 minutes is excellent, 90 seconds good, 60 seconds fair, less than 60 seconds poor.

Prone Hold Test

A stopwatch will be required for this test.

Procedure

Lay on your stomach with the elbows directly under the shoulders, forearms on the floor, legs extended, and your feet together.

Elevate your body into a standard push-up position.

Do not allow the hips to sag or elevate into the air.

Record the amount of time you can "hold" the correct position of the test.

A time of over 2 minutes is excellent, 60-90 seconds good, 45-60 seconds average, less than 45 seconds poor.

Functional Movement

Pitching is a total body athletic action requiring the entire kinetic chain from "feet to fingertips" to be functioning properly for efficient execution. We know from previous chapters the body works in an alternating pattern of mobile joints and stable body segments. The functional movement assessments listed below will help determine if the body as a whole is operating as a "unit" to create movement. The functional movement tests will look at how your body is accelerating, decelerating, and stabilizing during multiple planes of motion. In addition these tests will assess bilateral mobility of the ankles, hips, and shoulders.

Multi-Direction Lunge Test

Procedure

Begin this assessment by placing pieces of tape in the fashion of a large clock face on the floor. Set a piece of tape at the 12, 3, 6, and 9 o'clock positions of the clock face and stand in the middle. Place the hands on your hips, feet together, torso upright, and eyes looking forward.

Proceed to step forward to the 12 o'clock position with the right leg into a lunge position. Pause for one second at the bottom position of the lunge, return to the center point of the clock and repeat the lunge to the12 o'clock position with the left leg.

Once complete step laterally with the right leg towards the 3 o'clock position and perform a side lunge to the right. Pause for one second, return to the center point of the clock, and repeat a side lunge to the 9 o'clock position with the left leg.

Complete the assessment by stepping backwards into a lunge position with the right leg towards the 6 o'clock position of the clock. Pause for one second at the bottom position of the lunge. Return to the center position of the clock and repeat the backwards lunge with the left leg.

Once complete grade the level of difficulty of the assessment on a scale of 1 to 10 (10 being the most difficult). In addition record any difficulties in the completion of a lunge with either leg to any of the clock positions. A score of 1-3 is excellent, 3-5 average, 5 or above less than average.

Any differentiation between completion of the assessment by the left and right leg is an indicator of unilateral dysfunction in the kinetic chain.

Overhead Squat Test

Procedure

A dowel rod or similar object will be required for this assessment.

Begin in front of a full-length mirror, place the feet shoulder width apart, toes pointed straight, and hands grasping the dowel rod. Place the dowel rod on the top of your head and position the hands on the rod so that a 90-degree bend occurs in both elbows. Extend the arms straight overhead with the dowel round in-line with the head and over the feet.

Squat down as far as possible, keeping the dowel rod as high as possible overhead, pause for one second at the bottom position of your squat and return to the starting position of the assessment and repeat.

Discontinue the assessment if pain or discomfort is felt. Otherwise continue the assessment for a total of 10 repetitions. During the execution of the assessment, visually observe the ankle, knee, hips, torso, and shoulder joints.

A correctly executed overhead squat occurs when at the bottom of the squat: 1) the torso is upright and not leaning forward, 2) the arms are completely straight and dissecting the center line of body, 3) the upper leg is below parallel relative to the floor, 4) the knees are directly over the feet and not pressing outward or inward, 5) the feet are pointing forward and not flared outward, and 6) the heels are firmly on the floor.

Record the results of the assessment.

Utilize the information listed below to determine mobility and stability issues within the kinetic chain during the functional movement patterns of the overhead squat. A "yes" answer or "poor" marking points to a mobility or stability issue within the kinetic chain.

Table 1.4 Overhead Squat Assessment Chart

Ankle Range of Motion	Good	Poor
Knee Range of Motion	Good	Poor
Hip Range of Motion	Good	Poor
Shoulder Range of Motion	Good	Poor
Feet Rotate	Yes	No
Heels Elevate	Yes	No
Medial (Inward) or Lateral (Outward) Knee Tracking	Yes	No
Lower Back Arches or Rounds	Yes	No
Weight Shift Left or Right	Yes	No

Power

Power applied to pitching is measured by fast ball speed. The more speed developed by the pitcher within the mechanics of the throwing motion will equate to higher speeds on the radar gun. Power developed by the muscular system is one component of this speed. An assessment of the power outputs by your body can help determine how to improve your throwing speed. The assessments listed below will assist in determining your body's power outputs.

Jump Squat Test

Procedure

Begin by standing 4 to 6 inches away from a wall.

Place your feet shoulder width apart and arms overhead.

Begin the test by dropping down into a squat and explosively jumping as high as you can. At the highest point of your jump touch the wall.

Perform the test 3 times. Measure the distance from the floor to the point of your highest jump and record. your results.

Overhead MB Throw Test

A 4-6 pound medicine ball or similar object and a tape measure will be required for this assessment.

Procedure

Place yourself in a standard sit-up position (knees bent, feet flat, and lower back on the floor).

Grasp the medicine ball in your hands, overhead and resting on the floor.

Begin the test by performing an explosive sit up, throwing the ball forward over your knees.

Perform the test 3 times.

Measure the distance from your toes to the point where the medicine ball made contact with the floor, and record the distance.

Seated MB Throw Test

A 4-6 pound medicine ball or similar object and a tape measure will be required for this assessment.

Procedure

Sit on the floor, knees bent, feet together, toes pointed upward, and heels pressed into the floor. Grasp a medicine ball with both hands in front of your stomach.

Lean the upper body backward until your abs contract. Begin the assessment by rotating the torso as far as possible to the right. Pause at your farthest point of rotation for one second, and forcefully rotate towards the left releasing the medicine ball on the left side of your body.

Perform the test 3 times and measure the distance from your hips to the point where the medicine ball made contact with the floor, and record the distance.

Repeat the assessment to the opposite side of your body and again record your results.

Summary

These assessments provides you a valuable resource to understand and monitor your current levels of mobility, flexibility, balance, strength, endurance, and power as related to pitching and the athletic actions required in baseball. For accurate results, remember to take your time with the testing procedures. Keep in mind if you are uncomfortable in performing one of the above assessments feel free to move onto the next. The results of these tests will provide you with an excellent baseline of where to begin your training program, what areas of the body require attention, and what physical parameters necessitate development. Again, it is strongly suggested you re-test yourself every 6-8 weeks to track your progress.

Chapter Five

Functional Warm Up Exercises

All to often the pitcher will begin a practice with little or no time spent on preparation of the body. "Get loose" in the outfield is a common mantra for many younger players or "play some long toss" is another common phrase. Unfortunately, this type of mantra is more detrimental than beneficial in the bog picture.

Why, because the body is not ready to perform the activities of the pitching motion with a high level of efficiency. The body is just not ready to perform such athletic actions without a proper warm up. I like to use one of my mentors mantras from pitching coach Tom House who always stated you warm up before throwing not throw to warm up.

Pitching and fielding your position requires the entire kinetic chain to execute the athletic actions required in the sport. In order for this to occur: the joints of body must be mobile, the nervous system must be firing at a high rate of efficiency, and the muscles of the body need to be contracting and relaxing efficiently. These physical requirements cannot occur with a few swings of the bat or throws with the arm and ultimately require a functional warm-up of the entire kinetic chain (i.e. body).

A functional warm-up is very different than what many individuals believe to be a proper warm-up. Often times a warm-up is viewed as just a couple stretches for those "tight" muscles of the body. A functional warm-up may incorporate flexibility exercises, but goes well beyond this idea of just "stretching". A functional warm-up consists of a series of modalities too; improve mobility in the joints of the body, amplify firing rates of the nervous system, and increase the contractile properties of the muscular system.

A functional warm-up program for baseball consists of three different types of modalities. The first set of modalities myofascial release exercises are to improve soft tissue pliability. The second are active flexibility exercises. These exercises are geared towards improving extensibility in the muscular system and excitability of the nervous system. The final set consists of dynamic exercises to improve the contractile properties of the muscular system in multiple planes of motion.

I suggest spending 10 to 15 minutes on a functional warm-up prior to practice, playing, and at the beginning of your strength and conditioning program. A bio-foam roller will be required for a number of the exercises listed below, such a product can be purchased at most local sporting good stores or on the web. Once you have completed the warm-up exercises, your body will be ready to swing a golf club, you will be more confident in your golf swing, and ready to workout.

Functional Warm-up Exercises

Following is a list of functional warm-up exercises that should be an integral part of your training program. These exercises are to be performed with strict attention to technique. The speed at which each exercise is performed is of less importance than completing a full range of motion. Listen to your body when performing these exercises and if excessive discomfort is felt in any exercise discontinue immediately.

Calf Foam Roll

Goal: Decrease density of the calf musculature.

Starting Position: Place the foam roller on the Achilles section of your left leg. Extend the leftt leg straight, bend the right leg with the right foot flat on the floor, and hands next to your hips.

The Exercise: Slowly roll the foam roller up towards the knee. Press the leftt leg into the foam roll as you begin to move. Continue to move the foam roll over the entire calf and stop just below the back of the knee. Reverse the movement, and roll back towards the starting position of the exercise. Move up and down the calf of the right leg 3-5 times. Repeat the exercise with the right leg.

Tip: Discomfort will be felt in areas of the muscle that are "tight", when this occurs pause for 5-10 seconds on these "hot spots" in the muscle.

Quadriceps Foam Roll

Goal: Improve pliability of the quadriceps and hip flexors.

Starting Position: Lay flat on the floor with the right knee bent at approximately 45 degrees. Place the foam roll parallel to your body on the front of the left leg just above the knee. Extend the left leg straight and place both hands on the floor above shoulder height.

The Exercise: Slowly roll moving the foam roll up the front of the left leg towards your hip. Continue to roll until the foam roll is resting on the hip, return to the starting position of the exercise and repeat 3-5 times. Perform the exercise sequence with the right leg.

Tip: Roll up and down the front of the leg focusing on the quadriceps and hip flexors.

Hamstring Foam Roll

Goal: Decrease density of the hamstrings.

Starting Position: Place the foam roller under the knee of your right leg. Extend the right leg straight, bend the left leg with the left foot flat on the floor, and hands next to your hips.

The Exercise: Slowly roll the foam roller up towards the glutes. Press the right leg into the foam roll as you begin to move. Continue to move the foam roll over the entire hamstringand stop just below the insertion point of the glute. Reverse the movement, and roll back towards the starting position of the exercise. Move up and down the hamstring of the left leg 3-5 times. Repeat the exercise with the left leg.

Tip: Discomfort will be felt in areas of the muscle that are "tight", when this occurs pause for 5-10 seconds on these "hot spots" in the muscle.

Glute Foam Roll

Goal: Develop mobility in the hips.

Starting Position: Sit directly on top of the foam roll with your right glute in contact with the foam roll, bend the right leg, and place the right foot on the floor. Bend the left leg setting the left foot across your right thigh. Set both hands on the floor.

The Exercise: Sit your weight onto the foam roll through the right glute. Roll back and forth on the foam roll 3-5 times keeping the glute in contact with the foam roll. Again, sit on any "hot spots" for 5-10 seconds. Repeat the exercise with the left glute.

Tip: Rotate to your left and right to hit the entire glute.

IT Band Foam Roll

Goal: Improve pliability in the IT band.

Starting Position: Lay sideways with the right hip in contact with the foam roll. Extend the right leg straight, bend the left leg placing the left foot in front of the right knee. Place the right forearm on the floor with the elbow directly under your shoulder. Set the left hand on the floor in front of your chest.

The Exercise: Slowly roll down the side of the leg to your knee. Reverse direction and roll upward to the hip. Use the right forearm, left foot, and hand as the "driver" of the exercise. Roll back and forth on the IT Band 3-5 times. Pause on any tissue areas where discomfort is felt. Repeat the exercise on the left leg.

Tip: The IT Band tends to be "tight" on many individuals and as a result this exercise can cause discomfort. This discomfort should disperse after 2 weeks of foam rolling.

Adductors Foam Roll

Goal: Improve pliability of the adductors.

Starting Position: Lay flat on the floor with the left knee bent at approximately 45 degrees. Place the foam roll parallel to your body on the inside of the left leg just above the knee. Extend the right straight and place both hands on the floor above shoulder height.

The Exercise: Slowly roll laterally moving the foam roll on the inside of the left leg towards your hip. Continue to roll laterally until the foam roll is a few inches from the hip, return to the starting position of the exercise and repeat 3-5 times. Perform the exercise sequence with the right leg.

Tip: Roll laterally focusing on the inside of the leg to "hit" the adductors of the hip.

Thoracic Foam Roll

Goal: Improve density of the thoracic spine musculature.

Starting Position: Lay flat on your back, knees slightly closer than shoulder width, hands clasped behind your head, elbows next to the ears, and shoulders placed on the foam roll.

The Exercise: Slowly roll the foam roll down the upper back. Continue to roll until you reach the mid-point of the back. Reverse the exercise and roll upward to the shoulders. Alternate back and forth 3-5 times.

Tip: Keep the elbows next to your ears, and focus on the upper back.

Lat Foam Roll

Goal: Decrease density of the lats.

Starting Position: Lay on the right side of your body with the right arm extended straight. Place the foam roll directly under the shoulder joint of the right arm.

The Exercise: Slowly roll down the side of the body from the shoulder to the rib cage. Reverse the exercise movement back towards the shoulder joint and repeat 3-5 times. Repeat on the left side of your body.

Tip: Set your body weight into the foam roll and move slowly during the exercise.

Bent Knee Tennis Ball Lifts

Goal: Activation of the posterior chain

Starting Position: Lie with your back flat on the floor, knees bent, and feet together. Position a tennis ball on the anterior side of the left hip. Pull the left hip in towards your chest to secure the tennis ball in place.

The Exercise: Slowly press the hips upward by pushing the right foot into the floor. Continue to press the hips upward to a position inline with your right knee and shoulders while keeping the tennis ball in position. Pause briefly, return to the starting position and repeat for 10 repetitions. Repeat the exercise sequence with the tennis ball secured on the anterior side of the right hip.

Tip: Keep the tennis ball in position by pulling the knee into your chest.

Flat Bench Hip Extensions

Goal: Improve hip extension and activation of the posterior chain.

Starting Position: Place both of your hands on the floor directly under the shoulders. Position the hips in contact with the top of a flat bench, place both knees on the floor, eyes looking down to the floor and back flat.

The Exercise: Slowly press the right heel upwards, keep the knee bent and hips in contact with the bench. Continue to press the right heel upward until your right thigh is parallel to the bench. Pause briefly, return to the starting position and repeat for 10 repetitions. Repeat the exercise sequence with the left leg.

Tip: Keep the hips in contact with the bench throughout the entire exercise.

T-Spine Openers

Goal: Improve mobility in the thoracic spine

Starting Position: Place your hands and knees on the floor with hands directly below the shoulders and hips above the knees. Place the left hand on the back of the neck. Press the hips backwards towards the heels while keeping the right hand firmly planted on the floor.

The Exercise: Begin by rotating the left elbow towards the right arm. Continue to rotate until the left elbow comes in contact with the right arm. Pause briefly and reverse the rotation towards your left. Rotate the left arm, shoulder, and chest towards your left as far as possible while keeping the left hand in solid contact with the neck. Pause briefly and repeat the exercise sequence for 10-15 repetitions. Repeat with the opposite arm.

Tip: Keep the hand in contact with the neck through the entire exercise.

Wall Angels

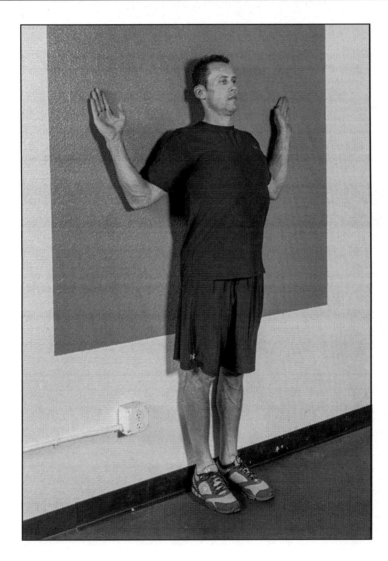

Goal: Improve thoracic spine mobility.

Starting Position: Stand upright next to a wall with the feet together, torso upright, and back pressed against the wall. Press both forearms into the wall with the hands flat and the bent. Position the elbows below the shoulders with the forearms angled outwards.

The Exercise: Extend the arms upward over the shoulder plane while keeping the hands and forearms in contact with the wall. Extend the arms as straight as possible while keeping the forearms and hands in contact with the wall. Return to the starting position and repeat for 10-15 repetitions.

Tip: Keep the back flat and forearms in contact with the wall throughout the entire exercise.

Bent Knee Side-to-Side Leg Swings

Goal: Improve mobility in the ankle and hips.

Starting Position: Stand 6-10 inches away from a wall, post, or cable column with the feet shoulder width apart, toes pointed directly at the wall, legs straight, hips facing the wall, and hands planted firmly on the wall at shoulder height. Lift the left leg off the floor, placing the knee in-line with the left hip.

The Exercise: Begin rotating the right leg in a swinging motion in front of the body. Keep the knee elevated at hip height and swing the leg left and right as far as possible while keeping the right heel firmly planted on the floor. Perform 10-15 swings of the right leg and switch to the right.

Tip: Keep the heel on the floor throughout the entire exercise.

Straight Leg Swings Side-to-Side

Goal: Improve mobility in the ankle and hips.

Starting Position: Stand 6-10 inches away from a wall, post, or cable column with the feet shoulder width apart, toes pointed directly at the wall, legs straight, hips facing the wall, and hands planted firmly on the wall at shoulder height. Lift the right leg off the floor.

The Exercise: Begin rotating the right leg in a swinging motion in front of the body. Keep the right leg straight and swing the leg left and right as far as possible while keeping the left heel on the floor. Perform 10-15 swings of the left leg and switch to the right.

Tip: Keep the heel on the floor throughout the entire exercise.

Straight Leg Swings Forward-Back

Goal: Improve hip mobility and flexibility of the hip flexors and hamstrings.

Starting Position: Standing perpendicular to a wall, post, or cable column, feet closer than shoulder width, torso upright, and left hand on the wall.

The Exercise: Lift the right leg a couple inches off the floor and begin to swing the leg forward and back, creating a pendulum motion. Swing the right leg forward and back as far as possible keeping the left heel on the floor and torso upright. Perform 10-15 repetitions and repeat with the left leg.

Tip: Keep your foot firmly planted on the floor throughout the exercise.

Sumo Squat

Goal: Increase mobility in the hips, extensibility in the hamstrings, and firing patterns in the lower body.

Starting Position: Stand upright, feet slightly wider than shoulder width, torso upright, toes pointed forward, and hands on your hips.

The Exercise: Begin by slowing reaching the hands towards your feet attempting to keep the legs as straight as possible. Continue to reach downward with the arms and hook the hands under your toes. Once complete, begin lowering the hips to the floor between the legs. Squat down as low as possible keeping both heels on the floor. Pause for 1-2 seconds at your lowest position and extend the hips upward keeping the hands hooked under the toes. Once complete, stand upright, and repeat for 10-15 repetitions.

Tip: Keep the heels on the floor throughout the entire exercise.

Single Leg Extension

Goal: Improve hip extension and glute activation.

Starting Position: Stand upright with feet together, arms straight, and torso upright. Lift the right knee off the floor bending the knee to a position in-line with the hips. Attempt to balance on your left leg throughout the entire exercise.

The Exercise: Slowly extend the right leg backwards while simultaneously reaching forward with both arms. Continue to extend the right leg and arms until straight and in a parallel position to the floor. Pause briefly, return to the starting position, and repeat for 10 repetitions. Repeat the exercise with the opposite leg.

Tip: Hinge at the hips and attempt to get the "long" in the exercise.

Forward Lunge with Reach

Goal: Dynamically warm-up the lower body and improve thoracic mobility.

Starting Position: Stand upright, feet together, arms resting at your sides, and eyes looking forward.

The Exercise: Step forward with the left foot into a lunge position. Plant the left leg on the floor, toes pointed forward, and torso upright, Lower your hips to the floor by bending both knees. Lower the hips to the floor until the left thigh is parallel to the floor. At the bottom position of the lunge elevate both arms overhead keeping the elbows straight. Pause for one second, lower the arms, and return to the starting position of the exercise. Repeat the exercise with the opposite leg. Alternate back and forth for 10-15 repetitions.

Tip: Keep the torso upright and extend the arms as high as possible overhead.

Side Lunge with Reach

Goal: Warm-up the lower body in a lateral movement pattern.

Starting Position: Stand upright, feet together, arms resting at your sides, and eyes looking forward.

The Exercise: Lift the leg up bending at both the hip and knee. Step to your left with the left foot. Plant the left foot on the floor, toes pointed forward, and torso upright. Bend the left knee, keeping the right leg straight, and torso upright. Simultaneously elevate both arms forward to shoulder height keeping the elbows straight. Continue to bend the left knee until the upper thigh of the left leg is parallel to the floor. Pause for one, return to the starting position of the exercise, and repeat the lunge to your right. Alternate back and forth for 10-15 repetitions.

Tip: Keep the heels firmly planted on the floor and toes pointed forward throughout the exercise.

Spider

Goal: Dynamically warm-up the hips, groin, glutes, and shoulders.

Starting Position: Place yourself in a standard push-up position, back flat, hands shoulder width apart, and eyes looking down.

The Exercise: Begin by lifting your left foot and placing it outside the left hand. Slowly attempt to press your left forearm down towards the floor, keeping your left hand in place. Lower your forearm as low to the floor as possible, and hold for one second. Return to the starting position of the exercise and repeat with your right hand and foot. Perform 10-15 repetitions.

Tip: Do not move the position of your hands throughout the exercise, keep a flat back, and do not lift your glutes towards the ceiling.

Summary

Remember, a functional warm-up increases mobility in the joints, increases excitability of the nervous system, and improves the firing rates of your muscular system. Again, I recommend performing this series of functional warm-up exercises prior to practice, playing, or the initiation of your strength and conditioning program.

Sample Pre-Practice /Pre-Game Pitchers Warm-Up:

Exercise:	Sets:	Repetitions:
1. Leg Swings Side-to-Side	1	10
2. Straight Leg Swings Side-to-Side	1	10
3. Straight Leg Swings Forward-Back	1	10
4. Sumo Squats	1	10
5. Single Leg Stationary Extensions	1	10
6. Forward Lunges w/ Reach	1	5
7. Side Lunge w/ Reach	1	5
8. T-Spine Openers	1	10
9. Tubing Internal/External	1	10
10. Tubing External Rotation at 90 degrees	1	10

Chapter Six

Flexibility Exercises

We know baseball requires a myriad of athletic actions to be performed during the course of a game. Not only are you asked to repeat the pitching motion, at times you will be asked to hit, bunt, field your position, and run the bases. We also know the entire kinetic chain is utilized in these athletic actions in multiple planes of motion. Knowing this and how the body operates in an alternating pattern of mobile joints and stable body segments, we can turn our attention to the concept of flexibility training.

The benefit flexibility training provides the athlete in conjunction with mobility is through the elongation of soft tissues (muscles, ligaments, tendons). Typically, certain muscles in the body are in a shortened position (i.e. "tight"), causing range of motion restrictions in their associated joints. The elongation (i.e. stretching) of these muscles through flexibility exercises will alleviate these restrictions allowing for proper ranges of motion to occur within the effected joints.

For example, "tightness" in the hamstrings is a common complaint for many athletes. If this is the case, the hamstrings are in a shortened position (i.e. "tight") pulling downward on the pelvis. This results in a mobility restriction within the hips that may cause difficulties in rotation or striding to home plate without injury. The repetitive pitching motion definitively fatigues the muscular system. Once the muscular system becomes fatigued the typical response after the conclusion of athletic activity is the "shortening" of muscle fibers. In order to return these fibers to optimal length for activity and speed the recovery process, flexibility exercises are extremely important. You can see from these simple examples how joint restrictions caused by "tight" soft tissues can cause problems within the body and the importance of flexibility training to alleviate such situations.

Flexibility Exercises

Delineated out below is a series of responsive flexibility exercises. The exercises focus on creating extensibility with the muscular system of the body. The exercises will address the musculature associated with the ankle, hips, thoracic spine, and gleno-humeral joint (shoulder) to allow for the mobility requirements of athletic actions. Perform each exercise in a passive manner, taking the target muscle(s) or joint through the suggested range of motion. In addition, pay strict attention to taking each exercise to the point of "tension" and holding the stretch for 30 seconds. Do not "bounce" during the execution of any exercise for this can result in injury. Technique is of the greatest importance with your flexibility exercises. Therefore pay strict attention to technique during the implementation of each exercise.

Back Press and Arch

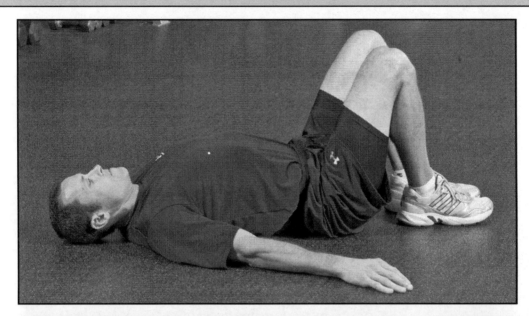

Goal: Extensibility of the lower back.

Starting Position: Lay with your back on the floor, knees bent, and feet together.

The Exercise: Round your lower back off the floor, maintaining contact of the hips and upper back with the floor. Hold this position for 30 seconds. Return to the starting position of the exercise and press your lower back into the floor for the 30 seconds.

Tip: Focus on arching your lower back off the floor.

Cats Down

Goal: Stretch the muscles of the lower back.

Starting Position: Place both of your hands on the floor directly under the shoulders. Position both of your knees directly under the hips, eyes looking forward and back flat.

The Exercise: Begin the exercise by rounding the lower back down towards the floor, simultaneously extending your head upward, keep the arms straight throughout the entire movement. Continue to round your back until a stretch is felt across the lower back. Hold the stretch for 30 seconds.

Tip: Think about arching your lower back downward.

Cats Up

Goal: Increase the flexibility of the lower, mid, and upper back.

Starting Position: Place both of your hands on the floor directly under the shoulders. Position both of your knees directly under the hips, eyes looking down and back flat.

The Exercise: Begin by extending your lower back upward towards the ceiling. Continue to arch the lower back up until it is rounded. Keep the arms straight throughout the exercise. Hold the position for 30 seconds.

Tip: Pull your pelvis upward during the extension of the lower back.

90/90 Hamstring Stretch

Goal: Stretch the hamstring complex.

Starting Position: Lay flat on the floor, knees bent, and lower back pressed to the floor.

The Exercise: Grasp behind the left leg with both hands just above the knee. Pull the knee into your chest. Straighten the left leg to a position where a stretch is felt in the left hamstring. Hold this position for the 30 seconds and repeat the exercise sequence with your right leg.

Tip: Do not "bounce" during the stretch and gradually straighten your leg.

Piriformis Stretch

Goal: Improve Mobility in the Hips.

Starting Position: Lay on the floor, knees bent at 90 degrees, feet flat on the floor.

The Exercise: Slowly place the outside of your right ankle on the thigh of the left leg. Grasp the right ankle with your left hand and place the right hand on the inside of the right knee. Elevate the left leg to a position where the lower leg is parallel to the floor and the knee is bent at 90 degrees. If an additional stretch is required, simultaneously pull with the left hand and press with the right hand until a stretch is felt. Hold the stretch for 30 seconds and repeat with the opposite leg.

Tip: Maintain a 90-degree bend in the knee when elevating the leg.

Glute Stretch

Goal: Increase extensibility in the glutes.

Starting Position: Sit on the floor with the right leg in front of your body. Bend the right knee to 90 degrees while keeping the hips facing forward. Place the hands on the floor slightly in front of the hips.

The Exercise: Slowly press the upper torso forwards towards the right knee. Keep the hips facing forward. Continue to press the torso forward until a stretch is felt in the right glute. Hold this position for 30 seconds and repeat with the left leg.

Tip: Press the chest towards the knee and do not round the back during the exercise.

Kneeling Hip Flexor Stretch

Goal: Increase flexibility in the hip flexors.

Starting Position: Kneel with the right knee in contact with the floor. Place your hands on your hips, and bend the left knee at 90 degrees.

The Exercise: Begin by pressing the hips forward, allowing your left knee to bend. Continue pressing forward until a stretch is felt in the right hip. Once a stretch is felt in the right hip, extend the right arm overhead, and bend the torso to the left. Hold the stretch for 30 seconds and repeat with the opposite leg.

Tip: Keep your torso upright.

Cat In-the-Wheel

Goal: Improve extensibility in the lats and thoracic spine.

Starting Position: Place both of your hands on the floor directly under the shoulders. Position both of your knees directly under the hips, eyes looking down and back flat.

The Exercise: Begin by extending your lower back upward towards the ceiling by lifting the hips. Continue to arch the lower back until it is rounded. Slowly pull your hips backwards towards the heels keeping the hands in place. Continue to pull the hips backwards until the glutes are resting on your heels. Hold this position for 30 seconds.

Tip: Keep the back rounded and hands in place throughout the entire exercise.

Seated Hamstring Stretch with Physio-Ball

Goal: Improve elasticity in the hamstrings.

Starting Position: Sit on top of ball, feet shoulder width, hands on hips, and torso upright.

The Exercise: Begin by extending the right leg straight, pointing the toe upward, and heel pressed into the floor. Slowly bend forward from the hips, pressing your chest towards the right knee. Continue to bend forward until a stretch is felt in the right hamstring. Hold this position for 30 seconds and repeat the exercise with your left leg.

Tip: Keep the torso upright and hinge at the hips during the exercise.

Quadriceps Stretch with Physio-Ball

Goal: Stretch the quadriceps and hip flexors.

Starting Position: Place the right foot and ankle on the side of the ball with the right knee in contact with the floor. Set the left foot on the floor in front of the torso with the knee bent at 90 degrees. Lean forward with the upper body and place both hands on the floor.

The Exercise: Slowly elevate the torso upward placing the hands on your hips. Maintain position of the both the left and right knee on the floor during the elevation of the torso. A stretch will be felt in either the right hip flexors or quadriceps. Hold this position for 30 seconds and repeat with the opposite leg.

Tip: Keep the hips facing forward and the feet shoulder width apart.

Lat Stretch with Physio-Ball

Goal: Improve extensibility in the lats and upper back.

Starting Position: Kneel on the floor, physio-ball directly in front of you, and hands on top of the ball.

The Exercise: Roll the ball forward by extending the arms and allowing your hips to shift backwards. Continue to extend the arms forward and your hips backwards until a stretch is felt in the upper back, lats, or shoulders. Hold this position for 30 seconds.

Tip: Keep your lumbar spine (lower back) straight throughout the entire exercise.

Physio-Ball Chest Stretch

Goal: Improve extensibility in the anterior shoulder.

Starting Position: Kneel on the floor, physio-ball placed directly next to your left shoulder. Place the left arm on top of the ball with the elbow bent at 90 degrees.

The Exercise: Slowly lower your chest to the floor by bending the right arm. Continue to press the chest downward until a stretch is felt on the front side of your left shoulder or chest. Hold this position for 30 seconds and repeat with the opposite arm.

Tip: Align the elbow with the shoulder joint and progress slowly with the pressing of the chest to the floor.

Posterior Shoulder Capsule Stretch

Goal: Improve range of motion in the shoulder joint.

Starting Position: Lay with the right hip in contact with the floor, legs straight, and the right upper arm perpendicular to the shoulder capsule. Bend the right elbow to 90-degrees so that the right upper arm in resting on the floor.

The Exercise: While keeping the shoulder capsule and right upper arm on the floor, grasp your right wrist with the left hand. Slowly press the right forearm towards the floor. Continue to press the forearm down until a stretch is felt in the right shoulder and hold for 30 seconds. Discontinue immediately if a pinch is felt in the right shoulder, and do not allow the right shoulder to elevate or roll forward during the exercise. Repeat with the opposite arm.

Tip: Pay strict attention to technique with this exercise, go very slowly with the pressing of the forearm and do not aggressively press the forearm to the floor.

Side Lunge Stretch

Goal: Increase flexibility in the groin.

Starting Position: Place your feet in a wide stance with both feet facing forward. Place your hands on the floor directly in front of your torso.

The Exercise: Lean the upper body towards the left foot, bending the left knee, keeping the right leg straight, and both heels on the floor. Continue to bend the left knee until a stretch is felt on the inside of the right thigh. Hold this position for 30 seconds and repeat to the opposite side.

Tip: Keep your back flat throughout the entire exercise.

Standing Calf Stretch

Goal: Improve flexibility in the calf musculature.

Starting Position: Place your hands on your hips, elbows bent, and body leaning forward. Extend your right leg backwards until it is straight, point your right heel forward, and bend the left leg.

The Exercise: Press your body weight forward by bending the left leg, keeping your right heel on the floor, and right leg straight. Continue to press forward until tension is felt in your right calf. Hold this position for 30 seconds and repeat with your left calf.

Tip: Keep your heel on the floor and back leg straight throughout the entire exercise.

Summary

The flexibility exercises in this chapter provide a comprehensive approach to developing extensibility in the musculature of the body for pitching. Remember the throwing motion requires mobility in the ankle, hips, thoracic spine, and gleno-humeral joint (i.e. shoulder). The musculature associated with these joint must be both pliable and flexible. Incorporate the above flexibility exercises in conjunction with the functional warm-up exercises in chapter 5 to accomplish this goal.

Sample Flexibility Program for Pitchers

Exercise:	Sets:	Repetitions:
1. Standing Calf Stretch	1	30 second hold
2. 90/90 Hamstring Stretch	1	30 second hold
3. Piriformis Stretch	1	30 second hold
4. Kneeling Hip Flexor Stretch	1	30 second hold
5. Glute Stretch	1	30 second hold
6. Cat in the Wheel Stretch	1	30 second hold
7. Posterior Shoulder Capsule Stretch	1	30 second hold
8. Side Lunge Stretch	1	30 second hold

Chapter Seven

Balance Exercises

The ability to create neuromuscular efficiency is integral to the execution of athletic actions. Recall from chapter two neuromuscular efficiency, commonly referred to as balance, is the ability of the neuromuscular system (nervous and muscular systems) to maintain the proper alignment, center of gravity, and coordinate the body during biomechanical movement. (Gray Cook, Athletic Body in Balance, 34) A pitcher who lacks neuromuscular efficiency will often execute athletic actions with less efficiency, placing greater amounts of stress on the body, and overall be less athletic.

Neuromuscular efficiency exercises (i.e. balance training) are based upon the principle of challenging an individual's limits of stability (balance threshold). Limit of stability is the distance outside one's base of support they can go without losing control of the kinetic chain (Michael Clark, Integrated Training for the New Millennium, 174). For example, if you were to stand with both feet on the floor with your eyes open, this would appear very easy to accomplish. Now if you lifted your left foot off the floor and balanced on one leg, this would be more difficult because you are now beginning to challenge the limits of stability of your body.

Through this process of challenging your individual limits of stability, improvement in your proprioceptive qualities and kinesthetic awareness occurs. This in turns improves the ability of the neuromuscular system to maintain proper alignment of the kinetic chain, maintain center of gravity, and coordinate movements. The concept of release point, knowing where your body is during the delivery, and recognizing when the mechanics of the delivery are "off" are all related to neuromuscular efficiency.

Balance Exercises

Below is a series of balance exercises to assist in the development of neuromuscular efficiency and stability within your body. The exercises will challenge your individual limits of stability as well as force the muscular system to produce force, reduce force, and stabilize in multiple planes of motion. Many of these exercises will require you to balance on one foot or maintain a specific posture while performing a corollary movement. As a result, it is strongly recommended to perform only the exercises within this chapter that you are comfortable performing and can execute with proper technique. I recommend performing your balance exercises after the functional warm-up and flexibility sections of your program.

Single Leg Balance

Goal: Improve kinesthetic awareness and balance capacities of the entire body.

Starting Position: Stand upright, hands on your hips, feet together and eyes looking forward.

The Exercise: Raise the left foot off the floor, bend the left knee 90 degrees and balance on the right leg for 30 to 45 seconds. Repeat the exercise balancing on your leftt leg.

Tip: Keep the upper body upright, and attempt to balance on a single leg for the entire exercise.

Single Leg Cone Reach

Goal: Improve neuromuscular coordination and lower body stabilization.

Starting Position: Place a towel, cone, or other object 2 to 3 feet in front of your feet. Place your feet together, hands on hips, and torso upright. Lift the leftt foot off the floor and balance on your right leg. Attempt to keep the left foot off the floor throughout the entire exercise.

The Exercise: Begin by reaching forward with the leftt hand towards the object in front of you, allowing the right knee to bend. Continue reaching until your hand is a couple inches above the object on the floor. Pause for one second at this point and return to an upright position maintaining your balance on the right leg. Perform 10-15 repetitions of the exercise and repeat on your opposite leg.

Tip: Stand upright between each repetition and allow the knee to bend during the exercise.

Single Leg Toe Touch

Goal: Increase proprioceptive qualities of the body and improve the hip hinge.

Starting Position: Stand upright with your feet together and hands on your hips. Raise the left arm overhead and lift the left foot a couple inches off the floor.

The Exercise: Reach with your left hand down towards the right foot. Hinge at the hip to create the movement. Continue to reach downward to a point slightly in front of your right foot. Keep your left foot off the floor throughout the entire exercise. At the bottom position of the toe touch pause for one second and return to an upright position continuing to balance on your right foot. Perform 10-15 repetitions and repeat balancing on the opposite foot.

Tip: Maintain balance on one foot the entire exercise and return to an upright position each repetition.

Single Leg Airplane Rotations

Goal: Develop lower body stability and improve balance capacities during rotation.

Starting Position: Place feet together, bend at the hip so the back is flat, and chest is parallel to the floor. Extend your arms straight out from the shoulders, lift the right foot off the floor, extend the leg straight, and balance on your left foot. Keep the right leg straight and off the floor during the entire exercise.

The Exercise: Begin the exercise by rotating your left arm downwards toward the left foot. Simultaneously rotate the right arm upward. Create the rotation in the upper torso of the body. Continue to rotate to a position where the left hand is directly above your left foot, and the right hand is pointing straight up. Return to the starting position of the exercise, perform 10-15 repetitions, and repeat on the opposite leg.

Tip: Keep your chest parallel to the floor, and try to maintain your balance throughout the entire exercise.

Balance Pad Single Leg Cone Reach

Goal: Improve neuromuscular coordination and lower body stabilization.

Starting Position: Place a towel, cone, or other object 2 to 3 feet in front of your feet. Place your feet together, hands on hips, torso upright, and standing in the middle of the balance pad. Lift the right foot off the balance pad, and balance on your left leg. Attempt to keep the right foot off the floor or balance board throughout the entire exercise.

The Exercise: Begin by reaching forward with the right hand towards the object in front of you, allowing the left knee to bend. Continue reaching until your hand is a couple inches above the object on the floor. Pause for one second at this point and return to an upright position maintaining your balance on the left leg. Perform 10-15 repetitions of the exercise and repeat on your opposite leg.

Tip: Stand upright between each repetition and allow the knee to bend during the exercise.

Balance Pad Single Leg Toe Touch

Goal: Increase proprioceptive qualities of the body and improve the hip hinge.

Starting Position: Stand upright with your feet together on the balance pad and hands on your hips. Raise the right arm overhead and lift the right foot a couple inches off the balance pad.

The Exercise: Reach with your right hand down towards the left foot. Hinge at the hip to create the movement. Continue to reach downward to a point slightly in front of your left foot. Keep your right foot off the balance pad throughout the entire exercise. At the bottom position of the toe touch pause for one second and return to an upright position continuing to balance on your left foot. Perform 10-15 repetitions and repeat balancing on the opposite foot.

Tip: Maintain balance on one foot the entire exercise and return to an upright position each repetition.

Balance Pad Single Leg Airplane Rotations

Goal: Develop lower body stability and improve balance capacities during rotation.

Starting Position: Place feet together on the balance pad, bend at the hip so the back is flat, and chest is parallel to the floor. Extend your arms straight out from the shoulders, lift the right foot off the balance pad, extend the leg straight, and balance on your left foot. Keep the right leg slightly bent and off the balance pad during the entire exercise.

The Exercise: Begin the exercise by rotating your left arm downwards toward the left foot. Simultaneously rotate the right arm upward. Create the rotation in the upper torso of the body. Continue to rotate to a position where the left hand is directly above your left foot, and the right hand is pointing straight up. Return to the starting position, perform for 10-15 repetitions, and repeat with the opposite leg.

Tip: Keep your chest parallel to the floor, and try to maintain your balance throughout the entire exercise.

Side-to-Side Stabilization Hops

Goal: Improve proprioception in a dynamic movement pattern.

Starting Position: Place the feet together, knees slightly bent, hand on your hips, and torso leaning slightly forward. Lift the left foot a couple inches off the floor and balance on your right leg.

The Exercise: Begin the exercise by bending slightly downward on the right leg. Jump laterally to your left 2-3 feet and land on the left foot. "Hold" the landing of the jump on the left foot keeping the right foot off the floor. Pause for 3-5 seconds and jump back to your right foot again landing only on the right foot and keeping your left foot off the floor. Alternate jumping back and forth for 10-15 repetitions.

Tip: Focus on jumping laterally, do not concern yourself with the height of the jump, and attempt to "stick" each landing on the intended foot.

Single Leg Box Hops

Goal: Improve stabilization and your balance capacities dynamically.

Starting Position: Place a bench, plyometric, or step up box 4-6 inches in front of you. Stand with feet together, arms resting at your sides, and body upright. Lift the right foot a couple inches off the floor and balance on your left foot.

The Exercise: Extend the arms slightly backwards and bend the left knee slightly while maintaining balance on the left leg. Hop upwards on to the bench or box landing on the left foot. Absorb the landing by bending the left knee and attempt to maintain balance of the left foot. Pause for 2 seconds, step down off the bench, and repeat the hop with the left leg for 10-15 repetitions. Repeat the exercise with while balancing on the right leg.

Tip: Utilize a bench no higher than mid-shin level for this exercise and absorb the landing with a bending of the knee.

Summary

The implementation of balance exercises into your strength and conditioning program will improve the neuromuscular efficiencies of your entire body. Perform your balance after a proper warm-up and flexibility program. Over time you will begin to feel improvement in the coordination of movements involved in the pitching motion as well as improved stability. The result will be a greater opportunity to execute athletic actions of the pitching motion more efficiently, know where your "body is in space", and in general be more athletic.

Chapter Eight

Pillar Strength Exercises

Every ball player from little league to the big leagues must be aware of the necessity for certain segments of the body to be stable in order to execute the athletic actions required in the sport of baseball. Going back to our mobility/stability model of the kinetic chain, we are aware of the need to develop stability in the knee, pelvis/sacral/lumbar spine (hips/abdominals/lower back), scapular/thoracic spine (shoulder blades), cervical spine (neck), and elbow joints.

The development of stability within these joints/segments of the body allows an athlete to generate arm speed, transfer speed to the release point efficiently, maintain an efficient pitching motion into the late innings, and reduce the potential for injury. If an individual is lacking stability in any of these segments of the body, the ability to execute the athletic actions involved in the sport of baseball will be less than optimal.

As stated in chapter two, stability hinges upon the development of strength in the muscular system. In order to develop strength it is necessary to implement resistant training exercises into the strength and conditioning program. Resistance training overloads the muscles of the body, and over time, results in increased levels of muscular strength and endurance.

It is important to note resistance training is often misconstrued and thought of as only weight training exercises with barbells and dumbbells. Although it is true resistance training can incorporate barbell and dumbbell exercises, it goes well beyond this compartmentalized thought process. Remember, resistance training is any form of exercise overloading the neuromuscular system of the body causing adaptation over time. That being said, we must expand on this thought process of resistance training to incorporate additional modalities such as body weight training, elastic tubing exercises, medicine ball drills, plyometrics, vibration technology and much more.

This is a very important concept to understand relative to the athlete. Often times, especially the younger player will not be physically ready for the implementation of external resistance in the form of barbells and dumbbells. In these types of situations the implementation of resistance training in forms other than barbells and dumbbells are required.

Torso Stability

Developing stability (i.e. strength) for pitching begins within the torso of the body. The torso is a reference to the neuromuscular structure of the hips, abdominals, lower back, obliques, and scapulas (upper back), and shoulder joint. Due to the stresses placed upon the upper torso (i.e. scapular, rotator cuff, and shoulder complex) in the pitching motion a separate chapter is dedicated to exercises for this portion of the torso.

The torso often referred to as the core or pillar of the body is the focal point of athletic movement patterns. This anatomical area is responsible for a number of athletic actions in the sport of baseball such as the generation of rotary speed in the hips, the transfer of power generated in the lower body to the upper body, and the throwing motion. If the torso is unstable and weak, the ability to transfer this speed through the kinetic chain will be less than optimal, rotary speed can be less than optimal, and arm issues can all be a concern. That being said, the torso is an extremely important section of the body for the baseball player and pitcher to condition.

Torso Stability Exercises

It is important to keep in mind the principle of progression during the implementation of torso stability exercises. Relative to most ball players new to strength and conditioning programs I suggest beginning with bodyweight orientated exercises, progress to elastic tubing, physio-ball, medicine ball exercises, and eventually to more challenging exercises.

The torso stability exercises found within this chapter will address strength and endurance development in the hips and core complex. I recommend performing your torso stability exercises for strength and endurance development 3 to 4 days per week. Input your stability exercises after the warm-up, flexibility, and balance sections of your program. One to three sets of each exercise and 8 to 15 repetitions per set is ideal. As with all the other sections of your program, tailor the exercises within your core training to your individual needs, pay strict attention to technique, and safety is always first.

Bent Knee Back Hold

Goal: Develop postural strength in the lower back.

Starting Position: Lay with your back flat on the floor, knees bent, and feet together.

The Exercise: Elevate your hips off the floor inline with your knees and shoulders. Do not arch the lower back or allow the hips to sag. Squeeze your glutes and hold this position for 30-60 seconds.

Tip: Think about drawing a straight line from the shoulders to knees with your hips intersecting the line.

Prone Hold

Goal: Strengthen the abdominals of the core.

Starting Position: Lay on your stomach with the elbows directly under the shoulders, forearms on the floor, legs extended, and feet together.

The Exercise: Elevate your body into a standard push-up position. The hips should be directly in line with the shoulders and ankles. Do not allow the hips to sag or elevate up into the air. Hold the "push-up" position for 30-60 seconds.

Tip: Squeeze your glutes and think about your body being in a straight line from the shoulders to ankles.

Side Hold

Goal: Develop stability in the internal and external obliques.

Starting Position: Begin on your right side, elbow directly under the right shoulder, forearm on the floor. Extend your legs straight with the left leg on top of your right. Do not permit your elbow to placed in front of behind the shoulder on this exercise, doing so may cause discomfort in the shoulder capsule.

The Exercise: Elevate your hips off the floor to a position in-line with the feet and shoulders. Hold this position for 30-60 seconds. Do not allow the hips to sag. Repeat on the opposite side.

Tip: Keep the arm extended and eyes looking at your hand throughout the exercise.

Bent Knee Marches

Goal: Develop strength in the hips, glutes, and lower back.

Starting Position: Lie with your back flat on the floor, knees bent, and feet together. Point your toes upward by pressing the heels into the floor. Elevate your hips off the floor inline with your knees and shoulders.

The Exercise: Slowly lift the right heel off the floor maintaining a bend in the knee and hips elevated. Continue to lift the heel 12-18 inches off the floor, pause for one second, and return to the starting position of the exercise. Repeat the "lift' with the left heel. Alternate back and forth for 10-15 repetitions.

Tip: Keep your hips inline with the shoulders and knees throughout the exercise.

Hip Circles

Goal: Increase strength in the hips.

Starting Position: Place both of your hands on the floor directly under the shoulders. Position both of your knees directly under the hips, eyes looking down, and back flat.

The Exercise: Begin the exercise by lifting the right knee slightly off the floor with the knee bent at 90 degrees. Press the right knee backwards maintaining a bend in the knee. Continue the movement until the right knee is inline with the right hip. Slowly rotate the right knee outward in a circular motion completing the movement when the knee is returned to the starting position of the exercise. Perform 10-15 repetitions and repeat with the opposite leg.

Tip: Think about drawing an imaginary circle with the knee.

Side Leg Raise - Abduction

Goal: Improve strength of glutes and abductors.

Starting Position: Lie on your right side with head resting on the inside of the right arm. Extend both legs straight, toes pointed straight ahead, and left leg resting on top of right.

The Exercise: Raise the left leg upward in controlled manner. Keep the toes pointed and leg straight during the lift. Raise the left leg as high as possible, pause for one second, and return to the starting position of the exercise. Perform 10-15 repetitions and repeat the exercise set-up and sequence with the opposite leg.

Tip: Keep your toes parallel to the floor throughout the entire exercise.

Side Leg Raise - Adduction

Goal: Increase strength of adductors and hips.

Starting Position: Lie on your right side with head resting on the inside of the right arm. Extend the right leg straight and toes pointed. Bend the left leg, placing the foot in front of your right knee.

The Exercise: Lift the right leg upward in a controlled manner. Keep the toes pointed and leg straight during the lift. Raise the right leg as high as possible, pause for one second, and return to the starting position of the exercise. Perform 10-15 repetitions and repeat the exercise set-up and sequence with the opposite leg.

Tip: Lift the leg upward using the muscles on the inside of your leg.

Tubing Psoas Press

Goal: Increase stability in the hips.

Starting Position: Place an elastic mini-band around the feet, lie flat on the back, knees bent, and arms on the floor.

The Exercise: Elevate legs off the floor and bend the knees to 90 degrees. Simultaneously press the left heel forward and pull the right knee inward, creating tension on the tubing. Pull the right knee inward past the hips and press the left heel outward forward of the glutes. Pause for 5 seconds and reverse the movement. Alternate back and forth for 5-10 repetitions.

Tip: Keep the hips and lower back on the floor throughout the exercise.

Clam Shells

Goal: Develop strength in the glutes.

Starting Position: Place an elastic mini-band around both legs just below the knees. Lie directly against a wall with the right hip in contact with the floor, knees bent at 45 degrees, left leg on top of right, feet flat on the wall, and lower back pressed against the wall.

The Exercise: Slowly press upward with the left leg, elevating it 3-5 inches above the right leg. Pause for 5 seconds, return to the starting position and repeat for 5-10 repetitions. Create the movement with the hips, and do not allow the lower back or hips to come off the wall. Repeat with the opposite leg.

Tip: Keep the feet and glutes in contact with the wall.

Tennis Ball Lifts with Medicine Ball

Goal: Activate and develop strength in the glutes.

Starting Position: Lie with your back flat on the floor, knees bent, and feet together. Position the right foot on top of a medicine ball. Place a tennis ball on the front side of the left hip and pull the left knee in towards your chest. Continue to pull the left knee towards your chest until the tennis ball is secured in the hip.

The Exercise: Slowly elevate the hips off the floor by pressing through the right foot into the medicine ball. During the elevation of the hips keep the left knee pressed towards your chest and the tennis ball in place. Continue to elevate the hips upward to a position inline with your shoulders and right knee. Return to the starting position of the exercise, keeping the tennis in position and repeat for 10-15 repetitions. Repeat the exercise with the tennis ball positioned in the front of the right hip and left foot on top of a medicine ball

Tip: Focus on keeping the tennis ball in position throughout the entire exercise.

Mountain Climber with Bosu Ball

Goal: Develop stability in the core musculature

Starting Position: Position yourself in a standard push up position, back flat, feet slightly closer than shoulder width, and hands positioned on the sides of the Bosu ball.

The Exercise: Lift the right leg slightly off the while maintaining a plank position with the body. Pull the right knee in towards your chest. Continue to pull the right knee in towards the chest as far as possible and pause briefly at the end range of motion. Slowly extend the right leg straight while keeping the foot off the floor. Pause briefly with the right leg extend and repeat the pulling of the knee inward. Perform 8-15 repetitions and repeat with the left leg.

Tip: Keep the body in a plank position and arms extended throughout the entire exercise.

Alternating Arm and Leg Extension

Goal: Improve strength in the lower back and hips.

Starting Position: Place both of your hands on the floor directly under the shoulders. Position both of your knees directly under the hips, eyes looking down, and back flat.

The Exercise: Simultaneously extend the left arm and right leg. Extend both the arm and leg until completely straight. Hold this position for one second and return to the starting position of the exercise. Repeat the exercise extending the opposite arm and leg. Alternate for 10-15 repetitions.

Tip: Maintain a "flat back" position during the entire exercise.

Jack Knife

Goal: Increase strength in the abdominals and hips.

Starting Position: Lay flat on your back, legs straight, arms extended, and hands clasped together.

The Exercise: Lift both arms off the floor and at the same time raise the left leg. Continue to raise the arms and left leg until both extremities meet directly above the hips. Pause for one second and return to the starting position of the exercise. Repeat the exercise elevating the arms and right leg off the floor to the same end position. Alternate lifting the leg and right leg for repetitions.

Tip: Focus on elevating your head and shoulders off the floor as high as possible during the exercise.

Side Press Up

Goal: Increase Strength in the obliques.

Starting Position: Lie on your right side placing your elbow directly under the right shoulder. Extend your legs straight with the left leg resting on top of your right. Extend your left arm straight up with the fingers extended, and eyes looking at your hand. Do not permit your elbow to be placed in front or behind the shoulder on this exercise, doing so may cause discomfort in the shoulder capsule.

The Exercise: Elevate your hips 2 inches off the floor to begin the exercise. From this position press your hips upward as high as possible and hold for one second. Return to the starting position of the exercise and repeat for 10-15 repetitions. Repeat the exercise with your left forearm on the floor.

Tip: Keep the arm extended and eyes looking at your hand throughout the exercise.

Cable Press Out

Goal: Develop anti-rotational stabilization strength.

Starting Position: Grasp the handle of a cable or tubing with both hands at chest height. Position the feet perpendicular to the cable column and step 2-4 feet away from the column. Separate the feet slightly wider than shoulder width, square the hips, and shoulders so that they are perpendicular to the cable column attachment. Bend the elbows and position the hands directly in front of your sternum.

The Exercise: Press the hands directly outward from your sternum, do not allow the hips or shoulders to rotate during the pressing motion. Continue to press the hands outward until the arms are straight. Pause briefly and return to the starting position of the exercise. Repeat for 10-15 repetitions and repeat in the opposite direction.

Tip: Do not allow the hips or shoulders to rotate throughout the entire exercise.

Kneeling Cable Chops

Goal: Increase stability in the core and develop rotary strength.

Starting Position: Attached a bar or rope to a cable attachment and lock in the highest position of the cable column. Position yourself in a kneeling position 2-3 feet away from the machine with the left leg forward and perpendicular to the cable machine. Grasp the bar with the left hand at the top of the bar with the thumb pointing down and position the right hand at opposite end of the bar. Maintain an upright torso position with the eyes looking forward.

The Exercise: Begin the exercise by pulling the left hand to your left shoulder allowing the right arm to extend in front of you. Pause briefly and then simultaneously push the left hand towards the floor in front your torso as the right hand moves upward to the right shoulder. Pause at this end position, reverse the sequence of movements returning to the starting position of the exercise and repeat for 8-15 repetitions. Repeat the exercise with the right leg forward in a kneeling position and right hand at the top of the bar or rope.

Tip: Keep the torso upright and stable throughout the entire exercise.

Kneeling Cable Lifts

Goal: Increase stability in the core and develop rotary strength.

Starting Position: Attached a bar or rope to a cable attachment and lock in the lowest position of the cable column. Position yourself in a kneeling position 2-3 feet away from the machine with the left leg forward and perpendicular to the cable machine. Grasp the bar with the right hand at the top of the bar closest to cable attachment with the thumb pointing up and position the left hand at the opposite end of the bar. Maintain an upright torso position with the eyes looking forward.

The Exercise: Begin the exercise by pulling the right hand to your abdominal region allowing the left arm to extend in front of you. Pause briefly and then simultaneously push the right hand towards the ceiling in front of you as the left hand moves down towards the floor. Pause at this end position, reverse the sequence of movements returning to the starting position of the exercise and repeat for 8-15 repetitions. Repeat the exercise with the right leg forward in a kneeling position and left hand at the top of the bar or rope.

Tip: Keep the torso upright and stable throughout the entire exercise.

Physio-Ball Straight Arm Side-to-Side

Goal: Develop stabilization strength in the lower back, glutes, and hamstrings.

Starting Position: Place your head and shoulders on top of the physio-ball with feet shoulder width apart on the floor. Elevate your hips into a position where a straight line can be drawn from your shoulders to knees. Extend your arms straight out from your shoulders.

The Exercise: Slowly roll to your left on the ball. Continue to roll to your left until the ball is directly under the right shoulder and the left shoulder is off the ball. Hold this position for one second and repeat the roll to the opposite side. Alternate rolling back and forth for 15-20 repetitions.

Tip: Maintain the elevation of your hips throughout the entire exercise.

Physio-Ball Table Top

Goal: Develop stabilization strength of the lower back, glutes, and hips.

Starting Position: Place the head and shoulders on top of the ball with feet shoulder width apart on the floor. Elevate the hips to a position horizontally in line with your knees and shoulders. Place your hands on both hips.

The Exercise: Extend the lower right leg outward from the knee. Continue to extend the lower leg until it is straight. Hold the extended position of the right leg for one second and return to your starting position. Repeat the exercise with the opposite leg. Alternate back and forth for 15-20 repetitions.

Tip: Keep the hips elevated throughout the entire exercise.

Physio-Ball Forearm Saws

Goal: Develop stabilization strength in the lower back, glutes, and hamstrings.

Starting Position: Position your forearms on top of the ball with the elbows bent. Position the body in a traditional plank position with the feet together, hips inline with the shoulders, and the back flat.

The Exercise: Slowly roll forearms forward away from the body as far as possible while maintaining a plank position. Return the forearms to the starting position of the exercise and repeat the movement for 10-15 repetitions.

Tip: Maintain the plank position of the body throughout the entire exercise.

Physio-Ball Russian Twist

Goal: Increase rotational strength in the core.

Starting Position: Place your head and shoulders on top of the ball. Elevate the hips to a position horizontally in line with the knees and shoulders. Place the feet shoulder width apart on the floor, extend the arms straight, and clasp your hands together.

The Exercise: Begin rotating to the left, allowing the ball to roll underneath your shoulders. Allow the eyes to follow your hands during the rotation. Continue to rotate to the left to the position at which your left upper arm is resting on top of the ball. Return to the starting position and repeat the rotation to your right. Alternate the rotation left and right for 15-20 repetitions.

Tip: Focus on creating the rotation with your core. Do not twist during the arms during the exercise, but rather rotate. To increase the difficulty of the exercise, grasp a medicine ball or dumbbell between your hands.

Physio-Ball Jack Knife

Goal: Create strength in the abdominals and postural muscles of the lower back.

Starting Position: Squat down and place your stomach on top of the physio-ball. Roll forward on the ball by walking your hands out into a push up position. Continue to roll forward until only the feet remain on top of the ball.

The Exercise: Hold the push up position and pull your knees in towards the chest. Continue to pull the knees forward as close as possible to your chest. Hold this position for one second, return to the starting position of the exercise and repeat for 10-15 repetitions.

Tip: Keep your back flat throughout the exercise and think of curling your knees in the chest.

Physio-Ball Back Press

Goal: Strengthen the glutes and lower back.

Starting Position: Lie flat on the floor, arms next to hips, and feet on top of physio-ball.

The Exercise: Slowly elevate the hips off the floor by pressing the feet into the ball. Continue to press the hips upward until a straight line can be drawn from the feet to the shoulders with your hips intersecting the line. Pause for one second, return to the starting position of the exercise and repeat for 10-15 repetitions.

Tip: Press the arms into the floor during the elevation of the glutes and lower back.

Physio-Ball Bent Knee Back Press

Goal: Develop strength in the hips, glutes, and hamstrings.

Starting Position: Lie flat on the back and place your heels on top of a box or bench. Place the heels next to each other, bend the knees to 90 degrees, and extend your arms straight out from the shoulders.

The Exercise: Brace the core and extend the hips upward by pressing into the physio-ball with your heels. Continue to press upward until the hips are inline with the knees and your shoulders. Contract the glutes while pausing for one second at the top position of the exercise, return to the starting position, and repeat for 8-15 repetitions.

Tip: To make the exercise more difficult cross the arms over your chest.

Physio-Ball Roll Outs

Goal: Increase strength in abdominals, lower, mid, and upper back.

Starting Position: Place both forearms on top of the ball with elbows directly under your shoulders. Place the knees on a balance pad resting your body weight on the knees and forearms.

The Exercise: Slowly roll the elbows forward allowing your upper body and torso to move forward. Roll the elbows outward as far forward as possible. Return the elbows to the starting position of the exercise and repeat for 15-20 repetitions.

Tip: Maintain a "flat back" position throughout the exercise and squeeze your abdominals.

Tubing Walks

Goal: Increase strength on glutes and abductors.

Starting Position: Place an elastic tubing loop around both legs just below the knees. Stand upright with knees slightly bent, feet shoulder width apart, torso upright, and hands on your hips.

The Exercise: Press the knees outward creating tension in the tubing. Hold this position throughout the entire exercise. Raise the left foot slightly off the floor and take a mini-step sideways to the left, keeping the right foot in place. Continue the exercise by taking a mini-step with the right foot towards the left. Alternate stepping left and right for 10-15 repetitions.

Tip: Keep the knees slightly bent and pressed outwards throughout the exercise.

Summary

Implementation of torso stability exercises is a crucial component of your strength and conditioning program for baseball. The development of torso strength will enhance your ability to generate speed, transfer power from the lower body to the upper, decrease the potential for injury, improve arm strength, and overall athleticism. I suggest performing a comprehensive torso stability program 3-4 times per week. It is best to implement postural strength exercises after your warm-up, flexibility, and balance exercises.

Sample On-Field Torso Stability Program

Exercise:	Sets:	Repetitions:
1. Prone Hold	1	30 second hold
2. Bent Knee Back Hold	1	30 second hold
3. Alternating Arm & Leg Extension	1	10
4. Side Press Up	1	10
5. Side Leg Raise - Abduction	1	10
6. Side Leg Raise - Adduction	1	10
7. Jack Knife	1	10
8. Tubing Walks	1	10

Chapter Nine

Joint Integrity Exercises

Pitchers from the big leagues down to little league are well aware of the importance arm health is to pitching successfully. It is very apparent in this day and age of the sport the number of arm injuries occurring at the major league level require a high level attention to arm care. Unfortunately in this day and age we are seeing more and more arm issues at a younger age which becomes increasingly alarming.

I refer back to one of my mentors and experts in the field of pitching Tom House to clarify reasons behind arm injuries. Since I've known Tom the formula for the prevention of arm injuries is a combination of functional strength, biomechanical efficiency within the pitching motion, and workloads. Tom has always said "you are only as strong as your weakest link and efficient as your poorest mechanic."

What does this statement clarify?

The less efficient a pitcher is with the throwing motion, the greater amounts of stress placed upon the body each and every pitch. The greater stresses placed upon the body, the more work is required from the body to pitch, and thus increases the potential for fatigue and potential injury.

Secondly, the throwing motion is a total body "feet to fingertips activity" as Tom would say. As a result the entire kinetic chain (i.e. body) must have the required levels of strength and endurance to execute the pitching motion over an extended period of time. If the kinetic chain is "weak" the ability to execute an efficient throwing motion will be limited thus leading to breakdowns, fatigue, and potential injury.

Recognizing these components we can understand the relationship between arm health, efficient pitching mechanics, and a need to develop the physical parameters of the kinetic chain to a efficient level. Finally, what is the equalizer in this equation?

Workloads is the equalizer. Workloads equates to pitch counts, side sessions, long toss etc. If the pitcher is weak the workloads must be adjusted. If the pitcher has poor mechanics workloads must be limited. Regardless of how functionally strong or biomechanically efficient you are with the pitching motion if the workloads become to high, fatigue will definitively occur and injury most likely to occur.

Research on the pitching motion indicates the stresses placed upon the shoulder complex are very high. Additionally the articular structure of the shoulder joint can be considered a complex mix of instability and stability where many of the "weaknesses" of the kinetic chain or "inefficiencies" within the pitching motion will "show up". This is typically due to the need for the muscles of the shoulder to work "overtime" every pitch.

As a result a strength and conditioning program for pitchers must recognize the common points of injury and address them accordingly. That is why we separate the shoulder complex and scapular region from our pillar strength training section and address these structures independently.

We typically hear of a rotator cuff program for pitchers and rightfully so as the anatomical structure of the shoulder joint requires the four muscles of the rotator cuff (supraspinatus, infraspinatus, teres minor, subscapularis) to stabilize the humeral head (upper arm bone) in the gleno cavity (shoulder socket) in addition to assisting in the abduction, adduction, elevation, and rotation of the arm.

A joint integrity program for pitches includes exercises to increase the strength and endurance within the rotator cuff and scapular region of the upper torso. Research capitulates the need for stabilization of the scapula to execute a repetitive throwing motion and as a result exercise to promote integrity of this region is required.

Joint Integrity Exercises

The joint integrity exercises found within this chapter will address strength and endurance development in the scapular region, shoulder complex, and rotator cuff. I recommend performing your joint integrity exercises for strength and endurance development 3 to 4 days per week. Input your joint integrity exercises after the pillar exercises within your program. One to three sets of each exercise and 8 to 15 repetitions per set is ideal.

Body weight, elastic tuing, physio ball, medicine ball, and light dumbbell protocols will comprise the joint integrity exercises found within this chapter. Sample joint integrity programs are found at the end of this chapter in addition to later chapters in this book.

Physio-Ball Wall Side-to-Side

Goal; Increase endurance within shoulder complex.

Starting Position: Stand parallel to a wall, feet shoulder width apart, legs straight, and torso. Position the stability ball on the wall directly in front of your chest with the left arm extended and left hand in the middle of the stability ball.

The Exercise: Slowly move the left hand in a lateral motion left and right while keeping the arm extended. Once you are comfortable with the movement of the exercise increase the speed of the lateral motion while keeping the hips square to the wall. Perform 8-20 repetitions of the exercise sequence and repeat with the right hand.

Tip: Increase the speed of the movement once comfortable with the exercise.

Physio-Ball Wall Down-Up

Goal: Improve stabilization capacities of shoulder complex.

Starting Position: Stand parallel to a wall, feet shoulder width apart, legs straight, and torso. Position the stability ball on the wall directly in front of your chest with the left arm extended and left hand in the middle of the stability ball.

The Exercise: Move the left hand in down and up movement pattern while keeping the arm extended. Increase the speed of the movement once comfortable with the exercise movement. Perform 8-20 repetitions of the exercise and repeat with the right hand.

Tip: Keep the hips square to the wall throughout the exercise.

Physio-Ball Circles

Goal: Develop shoulder and scapula stability.

Starting Position: Stand parallel to a wall, feet shoulder width apart, legs straight, and torso. Position the stability ball on the wall directly in front of your chest with the left arm extended and left hand in the middle of the stability ball.

The Exercise: Begin moving the left hand in a clockwise circle motion while keeping the arm straight. Increase the speed of movement once comfortable with the circular motion and perform 8-20 repetitions. Repeat the exercise in a counterclockwise motion.

Tip: Keep the arm straight.

Physio-Ball Figure 8's

Goal: Develop strength and endurance capacities of the shoulder complex.

Starting Position: Stand parallel to a wall, feet shoulder width apart, legs straight, and torso. Position the stability ball on the wall directly in front of your chest with the left arm extended and left hand in the middle of the stability ball.

The Exercise: Begin to draw an imaginary figure 8 on the ball with the left hand. Increase your speed of movement once comfortable with the exercise pattern. Perform 8-20 repetitions and repeat the figure 8 pattern in the opposite direction for 8-20 repetitions. Repeat the exercise sequence with the right hand on the stability ball.

Tip: Keep the hips square to the wall and the arm straight.

Two Arm Overhead Medicine Ball Throw

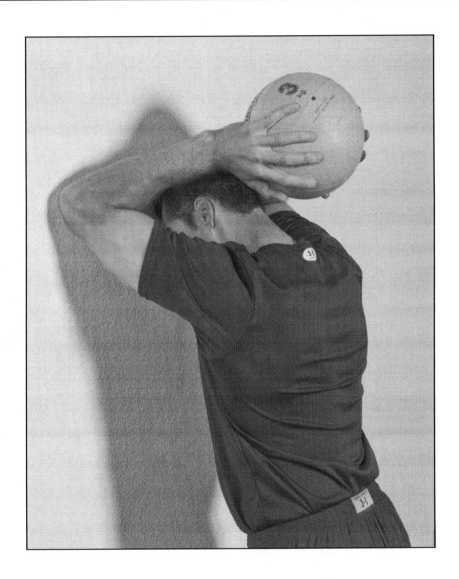

Goal: Increase endurance capacities of the shoulder complex

Starting Position: Stand upright, feet shoulder width apart facing a concrete wall with the arms overhead, elbows bent at approximately 30 degrees with both hands grasping a medicine ball.

The Exercise: Bend the elbows slightly allowing the medicine ball and hands to move to a position behind your head. Throw the medicine ball rapidly into the wall, catch the medicine with both hands, return the medicine to a position behind your head, and repeat the throw. Perform 40-50 repetitions of the exercise.

Tip: Create a rhythm with the throwing of the medicine ball.

Single Arm Medicine Ball Wall Throws

Goal: Develop endurance capacities of the shoulder complex.

Starting Position: Stand upright, feet shoulder width apart facing a concrete wall. Place a medicine ball in the right hand, bend the elbow 90 degrees, and position the elbow in-line with the right shoulder.

The Exercise: Throw the medicine ball rapidly into the wall while keeping the elbow in-line with the right shoulder. Catch the medicine ball with the right hand and repeat the throw with the right arm for 30-50 repetitions. Repeat the exercise with the opposite arm.

Tip: Keep the elbow in-line with the shoulder throughout the entire exercise.

Plank Scapular Push Up

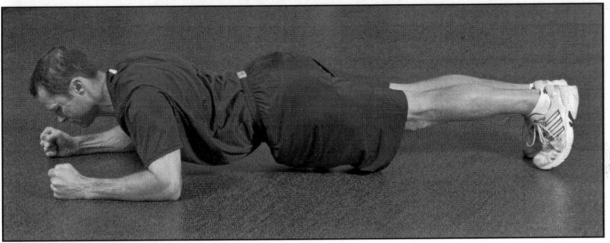

Goal: Develop scapular strength.

Starting Position: Lay on your stomach with the elbows directly under the shoulders, forearms on the floor, legs extended, and feet together.

The Exercise: Elevate your body into a standard push-up position. The hips should be directly in line with the shoulders and ankles. Do not allow the hips to sag or elevate up into the air. Hold the "push-up" position and "pinch" your shoulder blades together. Return to the starting position of the exercise and repeat for 8-15 repetitions.

Tip: Think about "pinching" a pencil between your shoulder blades.

Tubing External Rotation

Goal: Develop strength in rotator cuff complex.

Starting Position: Attach exercise tubing to a pole, cable column, or sturdy piece of fitness equipment at hip height. Grasp the exercise tubing handle with the left hand and step 2-4 feet away from the tubing attachment. Position your left elbow in contact with the rib cage and bend the left elbow to 90 degrees. Position the feet perpendicular to the attachment, shoulder width apart, torso upright, and eyes looking forward.

The Exercise: Externally rotate the left shoulder by pulling the left forearm away from the torso while keeping the left elbow bent at 90 degrees in contact with the rib cage. Continue to pull the left forearm away from the torso until the left hand is directly in front of the torso. Return to the starting position of the exercise and repeat for 8-15 repetitions. Repeat the exercise with the right arm.

Tip: Keep the elbow bent at 90 degrees and in contact with the rib cage during the entire exercise.

Tubing Internal Rotation

Goal: Develop stability in rotator cuff complex.

Starting Position: Attach exercise tubing to a pole, cable column, or sturdy piece of fitness equipment at hip height. Grasp the exercise tubing handle with the left hand and step 2-4 feet away from the tubing attachment. Position your left elbow in contact with the rib cage and bend the left elbow to 90 degrees. Position the feet perpendicular to the attachment, shoulder width apart, torso upright, and eyes looking forward.

The Exercise: Internally rotate the left shoulder by pulling the left forearm across the torso while keeping the left elbow bent at 90 degrees and in contact with the rib cage. Continue to pull the left forearm across the torso until the left hand is in contact with your rib cage on the right side of the body. Return to the starting position of the exercise and repeat for 8-15 repetitions. Repeat the exercise with the right arm.

Tip: Keep the elbow bent at 90 degrees and in contact with the rib cage during the entire exercise.

Tubing Shoulder Adduction

Goal: Develop strength in the shoulder complex.

Starting Position: Attach exercise tubing to a pole, cable column, or sturdy piece of fitness equipment at hip height. Grasp the exercise tubing handle with the right hand and step 2-4 feet away from the tubing attachment. Straighten the right arm and position your right hand inline with the right shoulder. Position the feet perpendicular to the attachment, shoulder width apart, torso upright, and eyes looking forward.

The Exercise: Adduct the right shoulder by pulling the right hand towards the right hip. Continue to pull the right hand downward until it is in contact with the right hip. Return to the starting position of the exercise and repeat for 8-15 repetitions. Repeat the exercise with the left arm.

Tip: Keep the arm straight during the entire exercise.

Tubing External Rotation at 90 Degrees

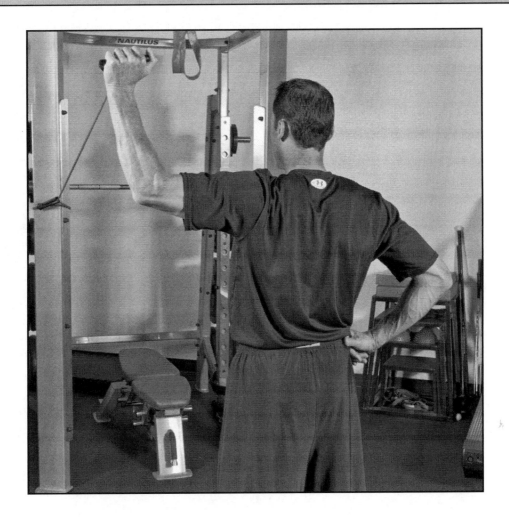

Goal: Develop strength in rotator cuff complex and scapular region

Starting Position: Attach exercise tubing to a pole, cable column, or sturdy piece of fitness equipment at shoulder height. Grasp the exercise tubing handle with the left hand and step 2-4 feet away from the tubing attachment. Position your left elbow inline with the shoulder, bend the left elbow to 90 degrees, and position the forearm parallel to the floor. Position the feet facing the tubing attachment, shoulder width apart, torso upright, and eyes looking forward.

The Exercise: Externally rotate the left shoulder by pulling the left forearm upward away from the floor while keeping the left elbow bent at 90 degrees. Continue to pull the left forearm backwards until the left hand is above the shoulder plane. Return to the starting position of the exercise and repeat for 8-15 repetitions. Repeat the exercise with the right arm.

Tip: Keep the elbow bent at 90 degrees and parallel to the shoulder throughout the entire exercise.

Kneeling Y's

Goal: Develop stability in the scapula.

Starting Position: Kneel on the floor, torso upright, eyes looking forward, hands grasping 3-5 lb. dumbbells, arms straight, and thumbs pointed upward.

The Exercise: Extend both arms simultaneously upward towards the ceiling. Keep the arms straight and the thumbs pointed upward. Continue to elevate the arms upward to a position over the head, pause for one second, return to the starting position of the exercise and repeat for 8-15 repetitions.

Tip: Keep the thumbs pointed upward and arms straight.

Kneeling T's

Goal: Increase shoulder stability of the torso.

Starting Position: Kneel on the floor, torso upright, eyes looking forward, hands grasping 3-5 lb. dumbbells, arms straight out from the shoulders, and thumbs pointed out to the sides

The Exercises: Pinch the shoulder blades together and extend the arms out the sides. Continue to raise the arms until a "T" is formed with the torso. Keep the arms straight and pull the shoulders blades together. Return to the starting position of the exercise and repeat for 8-15 repetitions.

Tip: Attempt to squeeze the shoulder blades together during the exercise.

Kneeling W's

.**Goal:** Improve scapular strength.

Starting Position: Kneel on the floor, torso upright, eyes looking forward, hands grasping 3-5 lb. dumbbells, arms bent, elbows slightly in front of your chest, and thumbs pointed upward.

The Exercise: Elevate the elbows upward towards the ceiling squeezing the shoulder blades together. Pause for one second, return to the starting position, and repeat for 8-15 repetitions.

Tip: Visualize a reverse pec dec machine movement.

Kneeling L's

Goal: Increase shoulder stability.

Starting Position: Kneel on the floor, torso upright, eyes looking forward, hands grasping 3-5 lb. dumbbells, arms bent at 90 degrees, and elbows directly inline with the shoulders.

The Exercise: Squeeze the shoulder blades together and simultaneously rotate both forearms upward towards the ceiling. Keep the elbows inline with the shoulders, and continue to rotate the forearms to head height. Pause for one second, return to the starting position of the exercise and repeat for 8-15 repetitions.

Tip: Do not allow the elbows to drop towards the floor during the exercise.

Summary

Developing endurance, stability, and strength within the rotator cuff, shoulder complex, and scapular region is imperative for the pitcher. I suggest performing a comprehensive shoulder/rotator cuff program 3-4 times per week. Listed below are sample programs.

Sample Joint Integrity Programs for Pitchers

Program One:

Exercise:	Sets:	Repetitions:
1. Physio-Ball Wall Down-Up	1	15
2. Physio-Ball Wall Side-Side	1	15
3. Physio-Ball Wall Circles Left-Right	1	15
4. Physio-Ball Wall Figure 8's	1	15
5. Plank Scapular Push Up	1	15
6. Tubing Internal Rotation	1	15
7. Tubing External Rotation	1	15

Program Two:

1. Tubing Shoulder Adduction	1	15
2. Tubing Internal Rotation	1	15
3. Tubing External Rotation	1	15
4. Tubing External Rotation at 90 Degrees	1	15
5. Kneeling Y's - T's - W's - L's	1	15
6. Two Arm Medicine Ball Overhead Throw	1	75
7. Single Arm Medicine Ball Throws Left/Right	1	75

Chapter Ten

Functional Strength Exercises

Up to this point we have provided you with a number of principles applicable to a pitcher specific training program, and the exercises to improve your arm health and performance. Information on balance, stabilization, torso, and joint integrity training have been presented in the last couple of chapters. These previous chapters of information make up the foundation of your training program. If any of the above mentioned areas of training are ignored then the outcome of your entire program will be less than optimal. We now turn to the functional strength training section of your training program.

We have discussed the importance of the kinetic chain, functional exercises, and cross specificity training. This is the point in your training program again where these principles are essential. We know pitching is a "feet to fingertip" athletic action where every muscle in the kinetic chain is being utilized either concentrically, eccentrically, or isometrically to create the pitching motion. We understand for optimal performance on the mound our training modalities must mirror the neuromuscular actions during competition (i.e. cross specificity training). This information brings us to the point where we are concurrently. We have created the foundation of our training program with modalities agreeing with these principles, but now what do we do to incorporate exercises training the larger muscles (i.e. prime movers) of the neuromuscular system?

Remembering the manner in which we train the exercises must be cross specific to the movement patterns associated with pitching. The above information should give you a pretty good clue. We need to train the kinetic chain of the body with multi-planar, multi-directional, isometric, concentric, and eccentric exercise. The exercises should focus on developing the neuromuscular capacities of endurance, strength, strength endurance, and power specific to the sport of baseball and pitching. Specific to the sport baseball refers to training the body a unit, not in isolated muscle groups because we know baseball is a sport in which the entire neuromuscular system is used to hit, throw, field, pitch, and run. As a result of this information we will be developing movement patterns incorporating the entire kinetic chain. This chapter will provide you the correct information and resistance training exercises for pitchers.

During the implementation of functional strength exercises, it is extremely important to follow the principle of progression (see chapter three). As stated previously, many younger players are not physically ready to be challenged with external resistance exercises in the form of barbells and dumbbells. Implementation of such exercises before the athlete is physically ready will detract from performance and increase the possibility of injury.

As a result it is best to begin the younger ball player with body weight orientated functional exercises, and progress accordingly. Simple guidelines of progressions for functional strength training exercises are as follows:

1) Commence with body weight training and advance to externally loaded exercises.

2) Begin with static (stationary) exercises and progress to dynamic (moving) exercises.

3) Start with slow exercise movements and advance to fast.

4) Initiate training with bilateral (i.e. two-legged, two-arm) orientated exercises and progress to unilateral (i.e. one-legged, one arm, or alternating arm/leg) exercises.

5) Begin training with low force output exercises and proceed to high force output.

Overhead Lifts for Pitchers

We are well aware of the stresses placed upon the body from the overhead throwing motion associated with pitching. As a result of this repetitive overhead motion it is imperative to touch upon overhead lifts for the lift. Questions arise about if these type of movements patterns are needed, if so what type of external resistance modalities are best for the pitcher, and what loads should the pitcher train with during overhead movement patterns?

Due to the stresses placed upon the pitcher during the throwing motion, knowing the necessary balance of elasticity, mobility, strength, and endurance required in the shoulder complex. Overhead lifts for pitcher can be of a benefit if performed with the correct technique, appropriate external loads, and equipment. Empirical evidence suggests not to use barbells in overhead lifts (i.e. military press), any exercises pushing or pulling behind the neck (i.e. wide grip lat pull downs), excessive loads, ballistic movement patterns (i.e. push presses), machine based overhead exercises (i.e. seated machine shoulder press), or exercises placing a loaded barbell on the shoulders.

Remember we have a large catalog of exercises to develop the functional strength parameters of the pitchers and eliminating the aforementioned exercises and modalities can be overcome with the proper program design. Secondly, the risk to reward ratio of these aforementioned exercises is just not worth the potential injury or performance concerns.

Functional Strength Exercises

Functional strength exercises are best performed 2-4 times per week dependent upon time of year, practice schedule, and throwing programs. Implement the functional strength exercises after the warm-up, flexibility, balance, torso stability, and joint integrity sections of your program. Functional strength exercises can cause extensive muscular fatigue. As a result, it is suggested not to perform functional strength exercises on consecutive days for the same movement patterns. Rather allow a recovery time of 48 to 72 hours for the body.

In addition it is best to select a comprehensive set of exercises from this chapter requiring the body to push (i.e. lower body squatting and upper pressing), pull (i.e. lower body and upper body pulling), and rotating during a single workout or consecutive workouts. Sample programs found in chapter 12 can assist you in this process of selecting the correct exercises to achieve this goal.

Body Weight Squat

Goal: Increase lower body push strength in the hips, glutes, and lower body.

Starting Position: Clasp hands behind your head and place feet shoulder width apart. Point the toes slightly outward and keep the heels on the floor.

The Exercise: Slowly lower the hips in a controlled manner towards the floor. Bend the knees to do so. Continue to squat until the thighs are parallel to the floor. Hold the bottom position of the squat for one second and return to the starting position of the exercise. Repeat the squat for 8-15 repetitions.

Tip: Keep the heels on the floor throughout the squat.

Jefferson Squat

Goal: Increase push strength on the lower body,

Starting Position: Grasp a dumbbell with both hands in front the hips. Extend the arms straight, place the feet slightly wider than shoulder width apart, toes pointed outward at 45 degrees, and heels on the floor. Maintain an upright torso with the eyes looking forward, and arms extended straight.

The Exercise: Slowly lower the hips while keeping the torso upright by bending the knees. Continue to squat downward until the thighs are parallel to the floor. Pause for one second, return to the starting position of the exercise, and repeat for 8-15 repetitions.

Tip: Keep the torso upright and heels on the floor throughout the entire exercise.

Goblet Squat

Goal: Improve push strength in the lower body.

Starting Position: Grasp a dumbbell with both hands in front the chest. Rest the dumbbell in the palms of both hands, and elbows pointing down. Place the feet slightly wider than shoulder width apart, toes pointed outward at 45 degrees, and heels on the floor. Maintain an upright torso with the eyes looking forward, and arms extended straight.

The Exercise: Slowly lower the hips while keeping the torso upright by bending the knees. Continue to squat downward until the thighs are parallel to the floor. Pause for one second, return to the starting position of the exercise, and repeat for 8-15 repetitions.

Tip: Keep the torso upright and heels on the floor throughout the entire exercise.

Kettle Bell Dead Lift

Goal: Increase push strength on the lower body,

Starting Position: Position a kettle bell on the floor between both feet. Position the feet slightly wider than shoulder width with the toes point slight out. Position the torso in an upright manner with the eyes looking forward, and arms extended straight.

The Exercise: Slowly push the hips backward and bend the knees while keeping the torso upright by bending the knees. Continue to squat downward until the hands are in a position to grasp the kettle bell. Grab the kettle bell with both hands keeping the arms straight. Pause slightly and begin extending the legs by pushing through your heels. Continue to extend the legs until standing upright. Squat down pushing the hips backwards and bending the knees. Continue to squat until the kettle bell contact the floor. Pause and repeat the extension of the legs. Perform 6-15 repetitions of the exercise.

Tip: Keep the torso upright and heels on the floor throughout the entire exercise.

Bulgarian Split Squat

Goal: Increase unilateral push strength in the hips, glutes, and lower body.

Starting Position: Place the left foot in front of the torso, knee slightly bent, and toes pointed forward. Set the right foot firmly on top of a step-up box or flat bench. Bend the right knee slightly, setting your body in a traditional lunge position. Clasp the hands behind your head, and set the torso upright with the eyes looking forward.

The Exercise: Set your core by contracting the abdominals, and descend the hips slowly towards the floor, bend both knees to do so. Continue to lower the hips towards the floor until the left thigh is parallel to the floor. Pause for one second and ascend slowly to the starting position of the exercise. Reset the bracing of the core and perform 8-15 repetitions of the exercise. Repeat the exercise sequence with the right leg forward and left foot on the box or bench.

Tip: Maintain an upright torso throughout the exercise.

Weighted Vest Bulgarian Split Squat

Goal: Develop unilateral push strength in the lower body.

Starting Position: Strap a weighted vest onto the torso. Place the left foot in front of the torso, knee slightly bent, and toes pointed forward. Set the right foot firmly on top of a step-up box or flat bench. Bend the right knee slightly, setting your body in a traditional lunge position. Clasp the hands behind your head, and set the torso upright with the eyes looking forward.

The Exercise: Set your core by contracting the abdominals, and descend the hips slowly towards the floor, bend both knees to do so. Continue to lower the hips towards the floor until the left thigh is parallel to the floor. Pause for one second and ascend slowly to the starting position of the exercise. Reset the bracing of the core and perform 8-15 repetitions of the exercise. Repeat the exercise sequence with the right leg forward and left foot on the box or bench.

Tip: Maintain an upright torso throughout the exercise and go to parallel with each repetition.

Dumbbell Bulgarian Split Squat

Goal: Increase single leg lower body strength.

Starting Position: Grasp dumbbells with both hands. Place the left foot in front of the torso, knee slightly bent, and toes pointed forward. Set the right foot firmly on top of a step-up box or flat bench. Bend the right knee slightly, setting your body in a traditional lunge position. Set the torso upright with the eyes looking forward.

The Exercise: Set your core by contracting the abdominals, and descend the hips slowly towards the floor, bend both knees to do so. Continue to lower the hips towards the floor until the left thigh is parallel to the floor. Pause for one second and ascend slowly to the starting position of the exercise. Reset the bracing of the core and perform 8-15 repetitions of the exercise. Repeat with the opposite foot on the bench.

Tip: Maintain an upright torso throughout the exercise and brace the core for every repetition.

Body Weight Step Up

Goal: Develop unilateral lower body strength.

Starting Position: Stand 4-8 inches in front of a step up box or flat bench. Place the feet slightly closer than shoulder width apart, toes pointed forward, torso upright, and hands clasped behind your head.

The Exercise: Step upward onto the bench with the left foot. Place the foot firmly on the bench with the toes pointed forward. Drive the body upward by extending the left leg. Continue to drive upward until the left leg is straight. Do not set the right foot on top of the bench at this point. Pause slightly and lower the right foot to the floor by bending the left knee. Keep the left foot on top of the bench and repeat the exercise for 8-15 repetitions. Repeat the exercise sequence with the right leg.

Tip: Focus on lifting the body with the leg that is on the bench.

Weighted Vest Step Up

Goal: Increase unilateral push strength on the hips, glutes, and lower body.

Starting Position: Strap a weighted vest onto the torso and stand 4-8 inches in front of a step up box or bench. Place the feet slightly closer than shoulder width apart, toes pointed forward, torso upright, and hands clasped behind your head.

The Exercise: Step upward onto the bench with the left foot. Place the foot firmly on the bench with the toes pointed forward. Drive the body upward by extending the left leg. Continue to drive upward until the left leg is straight. Do not set the right foot on top of the bench at this point. Pause slightly and lower the right foot to the floor by bending the left knee. Keep the left foot on top of the bench and repeat the exercise for 8-15 repetitions. Repeat the exercise sequence with the right leg.

Tip: Keep the body upright and focus on lifting the body with the leg on top of the bench.

Dumbbell Step Up

Goal: Develop single leg push strength in the hips, glutes, and lower body.

Starting Position: Grasp dumbbells with both hands, and stand 4-8 inches in front of a step up box or bench. Place the feet slightly closer than shoulder width apart, toes pointed forward, torso upright, and hands clasped behind your head.

The Exercise: Brace the core and step upward onto the bench with the left foot. Place the foot firmly on the bench with the toes pointed forward. Drive the body upward by extending the left leg. Continue to drive upward until the left leg is straight. Do not set the right foot on top of the bench at this point. Pause slightly and lower the right foot to the floor by bending the right knee. Keep the right foot on top of the bench and repeat the exercise for 8-15 repetitions. Reset the bracing of the core after every repetition. Repeat the exercise sequence with the right leg.

Tip: Keep an upright torso position throughout the exercise.

Single Leg Bench Squat

Goal: Develop unilateral strength and coordination in the lower body.

Starting Position: Sit on a bench, torso upright, hands resting on thighs, knees bent, and right foot slightly off the floor. Attempt to keep the right foot off the floor throughout the entire exercise.

The Exercise: Simultaneously extend both arms outward in front of the body and begin elevating the hips off the bench. Continue to lift the hips upward by straightening the left leg until the body is standing upright. Return to the starting position of the exercise and repeat for 5-10 repetitions with the left leg. Repeat the exercise sequence with the right leg.

Tip: Attempt to maintain balance on one leg and brace the core throughout the entire exercise.

Good Mornings

Goal: Develop hinging movement of the hip and develop strength in the lower body.

Starting Position: Place the feet shoulder width apart, hands on the hips, and torso upright.

The Exercise: Begin the exercise by slowly pushing the hips backwards. Simultaneously lower the chest towards the floor by allowing the knees to bend slightly. Lower the chest as close to parallel to the floor as possible while keeping the back flat. Pause slightly, return to the starting position of the exercise and repeat for 8-15 repetitions.

Tip: Add a weight vest for additional resistance and focus on hinging at the hips.

Medicine Ball Dead Lift

Goal: Increase pull strength in the hips, lower back, and hamstrings.

Starting Position: Grasp a 3-6 lb. medicine ball with both hands. Place your feet shoulder width apart, body upright, and hands resting at hip level.

The Exercise: While maintaining a flat back, hinge at the hips, bend the knees slightly, and slowly lower the medicine ball downward the front of your thighs. Keep your eyes looking forward and bend the legs slightly. Continue to lower the medicine ball to shin level in a controlled manner. Return to the starting position of the exercise and repeat for 10-15 repetitions.

Tip: Keep your back flat, and push the hips backwards during the descending portion of the exercise.

Dumbbell Dead Lift

Goal: Develop bilateral pull strength in the lower body.

Starting Position: Grasp dumbbells, place the feet shoulder width apart, torso upright, and hands resting at thigh level.

The Exercise: Brace the core by contracting the abdominals. Hinge at the hip and begin to press the hips backwards as you slowly lower the dumbbells down the front of your thighs. Allow the knees to bend slightly and continue to lower the dumbbells downward to just below the knees. Pause slightly, return to the starting position of the exercise by extending at the knees and hips. Repeat the exercise sequence for 8-15 repetitions.

Tip: Pay strict attention technique, do not overload the exercise, and focus on pushing backwards with the hips.

Barbell Dead Lift

Goal: Increase pull strength in the lower body.

Starting Position: Grasp the barbell with both hands at shoulder width. Place the feet shoulder width apart, torso upright, and arms extended.

The Exercise: Brace the core by contracting the abdominals. Hinge at the hip and begin to press the hips backwards as you slowly lower the barbell down the front of your thighs. Allow the knees to bend slightly and continue to lower the barbell downward to just below the knees. Pause slightly, return to the starting position of the exercise by extending at the knees and hips. Repeat the exercise sequence for 8-15 repetitions.

Tip: Pay strict attention technique, do not overload the exercise, and focus on pushing backwards with the hips.

Bent Knee Hip Extension

Goal: Develop strength in the hips, glutes, and hamstrings.

Starting Position: Lie flat on the back and place your heels on top of a box or bench. Place the heels next to each other, bend the knees to 90 degrees, and extend your arms straight out from the shoulders.

The Exercise: Brace the core and extend the hips upward by pressing into the bench with your heels. Continue to press upward until the hips are inline with the knees and your shoulders. Contract the glutes while pausing for one second at the top position of the exercise, return to the starting position, and repeat for 8-15 repetitions.

Tip: To make the exercise more difficult cross the arms over your chest.

Single Leg Medicine Ball Dead Lift

Goal: Increase single leg pull strength in the hamstrings, hips, and lower back.

Starting Position: Grasp a 3-6 lb. medicine ball with both hands. Place the feet shoulder width apart, body upright, and hands in front of hips. Lift the right foot off the floor and balance on the left leg.

The Exercise: Brace the core by contracting the abdominals and slowly reach with the medicine ball down towards the left foot. Bend at your hips and keep the left leg straight. Continue to reach with the medicine ball towards the top of the foot. Allow the right leg to extend backwards as a counterbalance. Pause for one second at the bottom position of the exercise and return to the starting position. Exhale at the mid-point of your ascent. Perform 8-15 repetitions and repeat with the opposite leg.

Tip: Attempt to balance on one leg throughout the entire exercise.

Single Leg Dumbbell Dead Lift

Goal: Increase unilateral lower body pull strength and improve balance.

Starting Position: Grasp dumbbells with both hands. Place the feet shoulder width apart, body upright, and dumbbell resting in front of hips. Lift the right foot off the floor and balance on the left leg.

The Exercise: Brace the core by contracting the abdominals and slowly reach with the dumbbells down to shin level. Bend at your hips and keep the left leg straight. Continue to reach with the dumbbell towards the top of the foot. Allow the right leg to extend backwards as a counterbalance. Pause for one second at the bottom position of the exercise and return to the starting position. Exhale at the mid-point of your ascent. Perform 8-15 repetitions and repeat with the opposite leg.

Tip: Attempt to balance on one leg throughout the entire exercise.

Single Leg Hip Extension

Goal: Develop single leg strength in the hips, glutes, and hamstrings.

Starting Position: Lie flat on the back and place your heels on top of a box or bench. Place the heels next to each other, bend the knees to 90 degrees, and extend your arms straight. Lift the left foot off the bench, keeping only the right heel on the bench.

The Exercise: Brace the core and extend the hips upward by pressing into the bench with your right heel. Continue to press upward until the hips are inline with the knees and your shoulders. Contract the glutes while pausing for one second at the top position of the exercise, return to the starting position, and perform 8-15 repetitions. Repeat the exercise using the left leg.

Tip: To make the exercise more difficult cross the arms over your chest.

Suite Case Dead Lift

Goal: Increase unilateral lower body pull strength and improve balance.

Starting Position: Grasp a dumbbell or kettle bell with left hand. Place the feet shoulder width apart, body upright, and dumbbell resting on the side of the left hip. Lift the right foot off the floor and balance on the left leg.

The Exercise: Brace the core by contracting the abdominals and slowly reach down the side of the left leg to shin level with the dumbbell. Bend at your hips, keep the left leg straight, and allow the right leg to extend backwards as a counterbalance. Pause for one second at the bottom position of the exercise and return to the starting position. Exhale at the mid-point of your ascent. Perform 8-15 repetitions and repeat with the opposite leg.

Tip: Attempt to balance on one leg throughout the entire exercise.

Tubing Row

Goal: Increase horizontal pull strength.

Starting Position: Stand upright, knees slightly bent, and eyes looking forward. Grasp tubing with both hands at shoulder height with both arms straight. Step 2-4 feet away from the tubing attachment to create resistance.

The Exercise: Begin the exercise by pulling both arms backwards by bending the elbows. Continue to pull backwards until the hands are next to both shoulders. Pause for one second and return to the starting position of the exercise. Repeat for 6-15 repetitions.

Tip: Maintain and upright torso throughout the entire exercise.

Tubing Press

Goal: Develop upper body horizontal push strength.

Starting Position: Stand upright, knees slightly bent, and eyes looking forward. Grasp tubing with both hands next to the shoulders and elbows bent. Step 2-4 feet away from the tubing attachment to create some resistance.

The Exercise: Simultaneously press the hands forward, keeping the elbows elevated and torso upright. Continue to press forward until both arms are straight. Pause for one second and return to the starting position of the exercise. Repeat for 10-15 repetitions.

Tip: Keep your elbows elevated at shoulder height throughout the entire exercise.

Physio-Ball Dumbbell Press

Goal: Increase upper body horizontal push strength.

Starting Position: Grasp dumbbells and lie with head and shoulders on the top of the ball. Place feet shoulder width apart on the floor and elevate hips to a position in line with your shoulders and knees. Place hands next to shoulders with palms facing your knees.

The Exercise: Extend your arms and press the dumbbells up. Continue to press upwards until the arms are straight. Return to the starting position and repeat for 8-15 repetitions.

Tip: Alternate the pressing of the arms to increase the difficulty of the exercise and always keep the hips elevated throughout the exercise.

Kneeling Dumbbell Overhead Press

Goal: Increase strength in shoulders, lower, mid, and upper back.

Starting Position: Grasp a dumbbell in the right hand and position the lower body in a kneeling lunge position with the right knee on the floor. Place feet shoulder width apart on the floor and eyes looking forward. Place the dumbbell next to your right shoulders with the elbow pointing down towards the floor.

The Exercise: Extend your right arm and press the dumbbell up. Continue to press until the right arm is straight. Return to the starting position and repeat for 6-15 repetitions.

Tip: Keep your torso upright throughout the exercise and do not lock your elbow.

Kettle Bell Single Arm Staggered Stance Row

Goal: Increase upper body horizontal pull strength.

Starting Position: Position the lower body in a modified lunge position with the right leg forward and left leg back. Bend the right knee to slightly less than 90 degrees and extend the left leg straight with the ball of the left foot in contact with the floor. Flatten the back, brace the core, and place the right hand on your hip. Position a kettle bell on the floor, and grasp the kettle bell handle with the left hand.

The Exercise: Pull the kettle bell upward towards your torso by bending the left elbow. Continue to pull upward until your hand is next to the rib cage. Pause slightly, return to the starting position of the exercise and repeat for 6-15 repetitions. Repeat the exercise sequence with the opposition hand.

Tip: Maintain a flat back and position of the lower body throughout the entire exercise.

Lat Pull Down

Goal: Develop upper body pull strength in the posterior chain.

Starting Position: grasp a pull up bar slightly wider than shoulder width with palms facing away from you. Extend the arms straight allowing the body to hang directly below the fixed bar.

The Exercise: Begin pulling upwards by bending both elbows. Continue to pull upwards until your chin is above the bar. Pause for one second, return to the starting position, and perform 8-15 repetitions.

Tip: Use the assistance of a spotter if needed to complete the suggested number of repetitions. Increase the difficulty of this exercise with a weighted vest.

Horizontal Pull Up

Goal: Develop upper body pull strength.

Starting Position: Grasp the lat pulldown bar slightly wider than shoulder width. Sit with knees bent, feet firmly on the floor, arms extended, and torso upright.

The Exercise: Pull the shoulders downward and shoulder blades together. Once the shoulders are "set in position" begin pulling bar downward towards the top of your chest by bending the arms. Continue to pull downward until the bar touches your chest at the collarbone. Pause briefly, return to the starting position, and repeat for 8-15 repetitions.

Tip: Maintain an upright torso throughout the exercise and use your back muscles to perform the exercise.

Single Arm Lat Pull Down

Goal: Increase horizontal upper body pull strength.

Starting Position: Place an Olympic bar on a squat rack at a height where you are able to hang underneath it. Lie flat on your back with the bar directly above the chest, legs straight, feet together, and torso rigid. Grasp the bar with both hands shoulder width apart pulling the body slightly off the floor.

The Exercise: Pull the upper body towards the bar keeping the feet in place and the legs straight. Continue to pull upward until your chest is touching the bar. Pause slightly, return to the starting position of the exercise and repeat. Keep the torso and legs straight throughout the exercise. Perform 8-15 repetitions of the exercise.

Tip: Increase the difficulty of the exercise by setting the feet on top of a bench or physio-ball. Always keep the body straight throughout the entire exercise.

Pull Up

Goal: Develop unilateral strength in the upper back and shoulders.

Starting Position: Grasp a single handle cable attachment with the right hand. Sit with knees bent, feet firmly on the floor, arms extended, and torso upright.

The Exercise: Set the right shoulder by pulling downward with the shoulder blade. Once the right shoulder is in a "set in position" begin pulling the right hand downward towards the top of your chest by bending the arm. Continue to pull downward until the handle touches your chest at the collarbone. Pause briefly, return to the starting position, and repeat for 8-15 repetitions. Repeat the exercise sequence with the left arm.

Tip: Maintain an upright torso, do not rotate right or left throughout the exercise, and use your back muscles to perform the exercise.

Single Arm Dumbbell Row

Goal: Develop unilateral upper body horizontal pull strength.

Starting position: Grasp a dumbbell with the right hand and place the left hand with the arm slightly bent on top of a bench. Set the feet shoulder width apart, knees bent, hips pressed backwards, and back flat. Extend the right arm straight while maintaining position of your body.

The Exercise: Pull the dumbbell upward towards your torso by bending the right elbow. Continue to pull upward until your hand is next to the rib cage. Pause slightly, return to the starting position of the exercise and repeat for 8-15 repetitions. Repeat the exercise sequence with the opposition hand.

Tip: Maintain position of the torso, hips, and legs throughout the entire exercise.

Summary

This chapter has provided you with the principles to follow in the set-up of your functional training program. Remember a pitcher specific conditioning program requires it to be: multi-dimensional, multi-planar, cross specific, progressive, systematic, and force output orientated. Functional strength training for baseball and the pitcher requires the development of lower body push, lower body pull, upper body push, and upper body pull strength. As a result it is imperative to utilize exercise developing all of the aforementioned strength planes. Listed below are some sample functional strength programs to provide you an idea of how to develop this section of your program.

Sample Functional Strength Programs for Pitchers

BEGINNER PROGRAM

Monday:	Lower Body Push - BW Squat	2 sets x 10 repetitions
	Upper Body Pull - Tubing Row	2 sets x 10 repetitions
	Lower Body Pull - Good Morning	2 sets x 10 repetitions
	Upper Body Push - Tubing Press	2 sets x 10 repetitions
Wednesday:	Lower Body Push - BW Squat	2 sets x 10 repetitions
	Upper Body Pull - Tubing Row	2 sets x 10 repetitions
	Lower Body Pull - Good Morning	2 sets x 10 repetitions
	Upper Body Push - Tubing Press	2 sets x 10 repetitions
Friday:	Lower Body Push - BW Squat	2 sets x 10 repetitions
	Upper Body Pull - Tubing Row	2 sets x 10 repetitions
	Lower Body Pull - Good Morning	2 sets x 10 repetitions
	Upper Body Push - Tubing Press	2 sets x 10 repetitions

INTERMEDIATE PROGRAM

Monday:	Lower Body Push - Jefferson Squat	2 sets x 10 repetitions
	Upper Body Pull - Wide Grip Lat Pull Down	2 sets x 10 repetitions

	Lower Body Pull - Medicine Ball Dead Lift	2 set x 10 repetitions
	Upper Body Push - Physio-Ball DB Chest Press	2 sets x 10 repetitions
Wednesday:	Lower Body Push - Bulgarian Spilt Squat	2 sets x 10 repetitions
	Upper Body Pull - Horizontal Row	2 sets x 10 repetitions
	Lower Body Pull - Med Ball Single Leg Dead Lift	2 sets x 10 repetitions
	Upper Body Push - Kneeling Lunge DB OH Press	2 sets x 10 repetitions
Friday:	Lower Body Push - Jefferson Squat	2 sets x 10 repetitions
	Upper Body Pull - Wide Grip Lat Pull Down	2 sets x 10 repetitions
	Lower Body Pull - Medicine Ball Dead Lift	2 sets x 10 repetitions
	Upper Body Push - Physio-Ball DB Chest Press	2 sets x 10 repetitions

ADVANCED PROGRAM

Monday:	Lower Body Push - Dumbbell Goblet Squat	3 sets x 8 repetitions
	Upper Body Pull - Wide Grip Pull Up	3 sets x 8 repetitions
Tuesday:	Lower Body Pull - Kettle Bell Dead Lift	3 sets x 8 repetitions
	Upper Body Push - Physio-Ball DB Chest Press	3 sets x 8 repetitions
Thursday:	Lower Body Push - Bulgarian Split Squat w/ DB	3 sets x 8 repetitions
	Upper Body Pull - Single Arm Dumbbell Row	3 sets x 8 repetitions
Friday:	Lower Body Pull - Single Leg Dumbbell Dead Lift	3 sets x 8 repetitions
	Upper Body Push - Kneeling Lunge DB OH Press	3 sets x 8 repetitions

Chapter Eleven

Power Exercises

Power in the most basic of formulas is strength plus speed. It is the combination of these two entities cohesively working together that allows a sprinter to sprint fast, a pitcher to throw hard, and a hitter to swing with power. The scientific definition of power states it is the ability to generate the greatest amount of force in a short amount of time. (Vladimir Zatsiorosky, Professor Department of Exercise and Sport Science, Pennsylvania State University)

Power pitcher, or a power slider are example of terms used with pitcher's coinciding with the concept. Basically both of these terms are connected to the concept of speed which is a result of power development within the kinetic chain. Relative to the biomechanics of the pitching motion we understand throwing velocity is developed through a step by step process from the "ground up" where each segment of the body adds speed up until release point.

Recognizing this biomechanical absolutes of the pitching motion and the basic formula of power (strength + speed) we can see the how power development can benefit the pitcher if the correct modalities and exercises are implemented into the pitcher's strength and conditioning program.

That being said, empirical evidence indicates not all forms of power training are conducive to the pitcher. Power training modalities are typically classified as plyometrics, jump training, med ball, or Olympic lifting, and Olympic hybrids. Referring back the risk-reward ratio of overhead movements for the pitcher, Olympic lifts, hybrids, and other overhead lifts may not be the most conducive for this population. Utilizing plyometrics and med ball training appears to be best for the pitcher in the development of power.

Power Exercises

The following power exercises for pitchers are categorized into beginner, intermediate, and advanced. I recommend training approximately 6 to 8 weeks at each level before advancing to the next. The table below lists power drills in relation to the level of difficulty. Keep in mind the physical requirements (i.e. flexibility, balance, strength) needed before the implementation of these exercises. As a pitchers perform your warm-up, flexibility, and balance exercises prior to your power exercises. This will assure your body is prepared to execute the exercises in this segment of your training program.

Table 1.4 Power Drills for Pitchers

BEGINNER POWER DRILLS

1. Kneeling Medicine Ball Side Throw

2. Kneeling Over Head Medicine Ball Throw

3. Box Jump

INTERMEDIATE POWER DRILLS

1. Front Twist Throw

2. Medicine Ball Side Throw

3. Overhead Medicine Ball Throw

4. Chest Pass

5. Scoop Throw

6. Hurdle Jump

7. Lateral Jump

ADVANCED POWER DRILLS

1. Single Leg Front Twist Throw

2. Side Throw Long Response

3. Overhead Step Throw

4. Step Chest Pass

5. Overhead Scoop Throw

6. Multi Hurdle Jumps

Beginner Power Exercises

A series of beginner power exercises for pitchers are listed below. Keep in mind it is best to develop adequate levels of flexibility, balance, and strength before the implementation of these exercises. Adhere to proper technique with the execution of each exercise. Perform only the number of repetitions you can perform correctly, and utilize the sample programs in chapter twelve for assistance. Perform one to three sets of each exercise two times per week.

Kneeling Medicine Ball Side Throw

Goal: Increase rotary speed of the body.

Starting Position: Grasp a 3-8 lb. medicine ball in both hands. Kneel in a parallel body position 2-3 feet away from a concrete wall. Rotate the torso away from the wall and set the medicine ball next to hip furthest away from the wall.

The Exercise: Rotate the torso explosively towards the wall, keeping the elbows slightly bent. Release the medicine ball into the wall. Catch the medicine ball on the return from the wall, rotate to the starting position, and repeat the throw of the ball into the wall. Do not pause during the exercise, but rather use the body's stretch reflex and rotational capacities throughout the exercise. Perform 6-8 throws and repeat in the opposite direction.

Tip: Utilize the torso and hips in the exercise and keep the arms passive.

Kneeling Overhead Medicine Ball Throw

Goal: Improve upper body power outputs and stabilization capacities of the torso.

Starting Position: Kneel facing a concrete wall. Position the knees 1-2 feet away from the wall, torso upright, arms straight overhead, and hands grasping a 3-8 lb. medicine ball.

The Exercise: Throw the medicine ball into the wall with both arms. Keep the torso upright and extended during the throw. Catch the medicine ball on the return from the wall, and repeat the throw of the ball into the wall. Perform 6-8 throws of the medicine ball into the wall.

Tip: Keep the torso upright and use the arms to throw the ball.

Box Jump

Goal: Increase lower body power outputs

Starting Position: Stand upright in front of a 6, 12, or 18-inch step up box. Place the feet shoulder width apart and approximately 1-2 feet away from the box. Bend the knees slightly, torso upright, and arms resting at your sides.

The Exercise: Bend the knees slightly, extend the arms behind the torso, and jump up onto the box with both feet. Land softly onto the box by bending both knees during the landing of the jump. Step back down off the box and repeat. Perform 6-8 jumps and pay strict attention to technique.

Tip: Beginners use a lower height box and advance to a higher box as you become more comfortable with the exercise.

Intermediate Power Exercises

Advancement to the intermediate level power exercises will require approximately 6-8 weeks of consistent training at the beginner level. The exercises found at the intermediate level will require more effort from your body. Pay strict attention to technique and perform only the number of repetitions you can execute correctly of the intermediate power exercises. Again, it is best to perform 3-4 sets of each exercise 2-4 times per week.

Table 1.5 Intermediate Power Drills for Pitchers

EXERCISE	EQUIPMENT REQUIRED
FRONT TWIST THROW	3-6 lb. Medicine Ball
MEDICINE BALL SIDE THROW	3-6 lb. Medicine Ball
OVERHEAD MEDICINE BALL THROW	3-6 lb. Medicine Ball
CHEST PASS	3-6 lb. Medicine Ball
SCOOP THROW	8-12 lb. Medicine Ball
HURDLE JUMP	12-36 inch High Hurdle
LATERAL JUMP	12-36 inch High Hurdle

Front Twist Throw

Goal: Increase rotary power.

Starting Position: Stand facing a concrete wall. Place the feet slightly wider than shoulder width apart and 2-3 feet away from the wall. Bend the knees slightly and grasp a 3-8 lb. medicine ball with both hands. Rotate the torso slightly and place the medicine next to the left hip.

The Exercise: Explosively throw the medicine ball towards the wall by rotating the torso. Aim the throw to a position directly in front of your torso. Maintain flex in the knees during the throw and generate the power from your hips. Catch the medicine off the wall and rotate the hips to your right. Continue to rotate until the medicine is directly next to the right hip and initiate the throw of the medicine ball back to the wall. Catch the ball return to the starting position of the exercise and repeat. Alternate throwing the ball from the left and right hip for 6-8 repetitions.

Tip: Maintain and upright torso and utilize the hips in the throw of the ball.

Medicine Ball Side Throw

Goal: Develop power in the hips.

Starting Position: Stand 3-4 feet away from a concrete wall. Stand with the feet shoulder width apart, and knees slightly bent. Grasp a 3-8 lb. medicine ball and place your hands next to the left hip.

The Exercise: Forcefully rotate your hips to the right, throwing the medicine ball against the wall. Allow the hips to rotate and your arms to fully extend. Catch the medicine ball and return to the starting position of the exercise. Do not pause during this exercise but utilize the body's stretch reflex during this exercise. Repeat the throw for 6-8 repetitions. Repeat the exercise sequence on the opposite side of your body.

Tip: Create a rhythm with the throwing and catching of the medicine ball.

Overhead Medicine Ball Throw

Goal: Increase upper body power outputs.

Starting Position: Stand facing a concrete wall. Place the feet 4-6 feet away from the wall, feet shoulder width apart, knees slightly bent, arms overhead, and grasping a 3-8 lb. medicine ball.

The Exercise: Bend the elbows and allow the medicine ball to move to a position behind your head. Allow the upper body to bend slightly backwards and then forcefully throw the medicine ball at the wall. Catch the medicine ball, return to the starting position of the exercise and repeat the throw for 6-8 repetitions.

Tip: Keep the feet firmly planted in the floor and allow to torso to bend forward during the throw.

Chest Pass

Goal: Develop power in the torso and upper body.

Starting Position: Stand facing a concrete wall. Place the feet 2-3 feet away from the wall, feet shoulder width apart, knees slightly bent, and hands grasping a 3-8 lb. medicine ball. Place the medicine ball directly in front of the chest.

The Exercise: Forcefully extend both arms throwing the medicine ball against the wall. Maintain an upright torso and slight bend in the knees. Catch the ball off the wall, return to the starting position of the exercise and repeat. Perform 6-8 repetitions.

Tip: Keep the torso upright and forcefully extend the arms with each throw.

Scoop Throw

Goal: Develop power in the hips and torso.

Starting Position: Stand facing a concrete wall. Place the body 6-8 feet away from the wall, feet slightly wider than shoulder width. Grasp a 3-8 lb. medicine ball with both hands in front of the hips.

The Exercise: Bend the knees, squat downward, allowing the ball to move in between the legs. Forcefully extend the hips forward and throw the ball forward towards the wall. Catch the medicine ball, return to the starting position of the exercise, and repeat for 6-8 repetitions.

Tip: Reset your body position between each throw and use the lower body during the exercise.

Hurdle Jump

Goal: Increase lower body power.

Starting Position: Stand directly in front of a 12 – 36 inch high hurdle. Place the body 1-2 feet behind the hurdle, knees slightly bent, torso upright, and arms resting at your sides.

The Exercise: Bend the knees and hips. Move both arms behind the torso and jump forward over the hurdle. Allow the arms to swing forward during the jump. Keep the body upright and generate the jump from the hips and lower body. Land softly on both feet and absorb the landing by bending both knees. Walk around the hurdle, place your body in the starting position of the exercise, and repeat the jump. Perform 6-8 jumps with proper technique.

Tip: Pay strict attention to technique, begin with a low hurdle, and advance to higher hurdle as you progress.

Lateral Jump

Goal: Develop lower body power.

Starting Position: Stand 1-2 feet to the right side of a 12-18 inch high hurdle. Set the feet in a lateral position to the hurdle, knees slightly bent, and arms resting at your sides.

The Exercise: Bend the knee, hips, and pull the arms backwards. Jump lateral and vertically over the hurdle. Land on the opposite side of the hurdle with both feet. Bend the knees and hips during the landing and immediately jump back over the hurdle to the starting position of the exercise. Alternate jumps laterally over the hurdle for 6-8 repetitions.

Tip: Allow the arms to move during the jump. Move both laterally and vertically during the jump.

Advanced Power Exercises

Once you have demonstrated expertise within the intermediate level power exercises, it is time to progress to the advanced level. The advancement to the advanced level typically requires 6 – 8 weeks of consistent training with the exercises found within the intermediate level. It is best to perform 3-4 sets per exercise 2-4 times per week of the advanced level power exercises.

Table 1.6 Advanced Power Drills for Pitchers

EXERCISE	EQUIPMENT REQUIRED
SINGLE LEG FRONT TWIST THROW	3-6 lb. Medicine Ball
SIDE THROW LONG RESPONSE	3-6 lb. Medicine Ball
OVERHEAD STEP THROW	3-6 lb. Medicine Ball
STEP CHEST PASS	3-6 lb. Medicine Ball
OVERHEAD SCOOP THROW	8-12 lb. Medicine Ball
MULTIPLE HURDLE JUMPS	12-36 inch High Hurdles

Single Leg Front Twist Throw

Goal: Improve rotary power and single leg strength.

Starting Position: Stand facing a concrete wall. Place the feet slightly wider than shoulder width apart and 2-3 feet away from the wall. Bend the knees slightly and grasp a 3-8 lb. medicine ball with both hands. Rotate the torso slightly, place the medicine next to the left hip, lift the left foot slightly off the floor, and attempt to balance on the right leg throughout the entire exercise.

The Exercise: Explosively throw the medicine ball towards the wall by rotating the torso. Aim the throw to a position directly in front of your torso. Maintain flex in the right knee during the throw and generate the power from your hips. Catch the medicine off the wall and rotate the hips to your right. Continue to rotate until the medicine is directly next to the right hip and initiate the throw of the medicine ball back to the wall. Alternate throwing the ball from the left and right hip for 6-8 repetitions. Repeat the exercise balancing on the left leg.

Tip: Maintain and upright torso and utilize the hips in the throw of the ball.

Side Throw Long Response

Goal: Develop rotational power in the hips and torso.

Starting Position: Stand 8-10 feet away from a concrete wall. Stand with the feet shoulder width apart, and knees slightly bent. Grasp a 3-8 lb. medicine ball and place your hands next to the left hip.

The Exercise: Forcefully rotate your hips to the right, throwing the medicine ball against the wall. Allow the hips to rotate and your arms to fully extend. Catch the medicine ball and return to the starting position of the exercise. Do not pause during this exercise but utilize the body's stretch reflex during this exercise. Repeat the throw for 6-8 repetitions. Repeat the exercise sequence on the opposite side of your body.

Tip: Explosively throw the medicine ball by generating power in the legs and torso.

Overhead Step Throw

Goal: Increase upper body power outputs.

Starting Position: Stand 6-8 feet away from a concrete wall. Stand with the feet shoulder width apart, and knees slightly bent. Grasp a 3-8 lb. medicine ball and place your hands above the head.

The Exercise: Bend the elbows placing the medicine ball behind your head. Step forward with the left foot towards the wall and throw the medicine ball at the wall. Catch the medicine ball, return to the starting position of the exercise and repeat the throw by stepping forward with the right foot. Perform 6-8 repetitions of the exercise.

Tip: Allow to torso to bend forward during the throw.

Step Chest Pass

Goal: Develop power in the upper torso.

Starting Position: Stand 6-8 feet away from a concrete wall. Place the feet shoulder width apart, knees slightly bent, and hands grasping a 3-8 lb. medicine ball. Place the medicine ball directly in front of the chest.

The Exercise: Step forward towards the wall with the left foot and forcefully extend both arms throwing the medicine ball against the wall. Maintain an upright torso and extend the arms. Catch the ball off the wall, return to the starting position of the exercise and repeat the exercise stepping forward with the opposite foot. Perform 6-8 repetitions.

Tip: Keep the torso upright and allow the ball to bounce on the floor before catching it on the return.

Overhead Scoop Throw

Goal: Develop total body power.

Starting Position: Grasp a 6-12 lb. medicine ball with both hands in front of the hips. Place the feet slightly wider than shoulder width apart, torso upright, and eyes looking forward.

The Exercise: Squat downward by bending at the both the knees and the hips. Allow the medicine ball to drop in between the legs. Lower the hips until the upper thighs are parallel to the floor. Explosively extend the hips upward and simultaneously extend the arms overhead. Continue to extend the hips until the legs are straight and release the medicine ball straight up in the air when the arms and legs are extended. Locate the medicine ball with your eyes in the air. Allow the medicine ball to fall to the floor, pick the medicine ball up off the floor, and repeat the exercise. Perform 6-8 repetitions of the exercise.

Tip: Visually locate the ball once it is released in the air and do not allow the ball to drop on your head.

Multiple Hurdle Jumps

Goal: Increase lower body power outputs.

Starting Position: Set 3 to 5 12-36 inch hurdles in a row. Separate the hurdles by approximately 2-3 feet. Stand directly in front of the first 12 – 36 inch high hurdle. Place the body 1-2 feet behind the hurdle, knees slightly bent, torso upright, and arms resting at your sides.

The Exercise: Bend the knees and hips. Move both arms behind the torso and jump forward over the hurdle. Allow the arms to swing forward during the jump. Keep the body upright and generate the jump from the hips and lower body. Land softly on both feet and absorb the landing by bending both knees. Immediately repeat the exercise sequence and jump over the second hurdle. Again, land softly, and repeat the exercise through the entire series of hurdles. Walk around the line of hurdles, place your body in the starting position of the exercise, and repeat the jumps. Perform 2-3 jumps through the hurdles.

Tip: Pay strict attention to technique, begin with low hurdles, and advance to higher hurdles as you progress.

Summary

This chapter has provided a series of power exercises. Remember it is crucial to develop a strong base of flexibility and strength within the body prior to the incorporation of these exercises into your golf fitness program. It is best to perform your power exercises 2-4 times per week depending upon your training program. Be sure to pay strict attention to technique in the execution of each power exercise.

Table 1.7 Off-Season Sample Power Programs

BEGINNER PROGRAM

Monday:	Kneeling Medicine Ball Side Throw	2 sets x 8 repetitions
	Kneeling Overhead Medicine Ball Throw	2 sets x 8 repetitions
	Box Jump	2 sets x 8 repetitions
Wednesday:	Box Jump	2 sets x 8 repetitions
Friday:	Kneeling Medicine Ball Side Throw	2 sets x 8 repetitions
	Kneeling Overhead Medicine Ball Throw	2 sets x 8 repetitions
	Box Jump	2 sets x 8 repetitions

INTERMEDIATE PROGRAM

Monday:	Front Twist Throw	2 sets x 8 repetitions
	Overhead Medicine Ball Throw	2 sets x 8 repetitions
	Hurdle Jump	2 sets x 8 repetitions
Wednesday:	Chest Pass	2 sets x 8 repetitions
	Scoop Throw	2 sets x 8 repetitions
	Lateral Jump	2 sets x 8 repetitions
Friday:	Front Twist Throw	2 sets x 8 repetitions
	Overhead Medicine Ball Throw	2 sets x 8 repetitions
	Hurdle Jump	2 sets x 8 repetitions

ADVANCED PROGRAM

Monday:	Single Leg Front Twist Throw	2 sets x 8 repetitions
	Overhead Step Throw	2 sets x 8 repetitions
	Step Chest Pass	2 sets x 8 repetitions
Tuesday:	Overhead Scoop Throw	2 sets x 8 repetitions
	Multiple Hurdle Jumps	2 sets x 8 repetitions
Thursday:	Single Leg Front Twist Throw	2 sets x 8 repetitions
	Overhead Step Throw	2 sets x 8 repetitions
	Step Chest Pass	2 sets x 8 repetitions
Friday:	Overhead Scoop Throw	2 sets x 8 repetitions
	Multiple Hurdle Jumps	2 sets x 8 repetitions

Chapter Twelve
Anaerobic Training, Aerobics, Nutrition, and Recovery

The previous chapters of this book have discussed the physical parameters required in the development of the pitcher. Areas to discuss in this chapter are the areas of anaerobic training, aerobic conditioning, nutrition, and recovery. It is interesting when we present these topics the thought which "pops" into most pitchers mind is running.

Running is a part of this equation and does serve it's purpose in the overall development of the pitcher but the real question is why do pitchers run so much?

You go back a few decades and talk to someone like Tom House about pitchers running so much in spring training and part of the reason was to keep the pitchers busy. You can only throw so much long toss, bull pens, and do PFPs, and you have to keep the pitchers doing something. There was more to it and as research has advanced we've become a little smarter about the entire equation.

Fast forward to my time in spring training and the pitchers still did conditioning though admittedly we had less of an aerobic thought process and more of an anaerobic or interval based philosophy. In this day and age I believe we have a found a good balance and understand the purpose of both aerobic and anaerobic conditioning for the pitcher.

Aerobic Conditioning

Aerobic conditioning can benefit any individual from little leaguer to MLB pitcher. Aerobic conditioning improves the cardio-pulmonary outputs of the body for health and wellness. Specific to the pitcher I steal a concept from my mentor Tom House and the benefits aerobic conditioning in the recovery process of a pitcher between starts.

The goal of aerobic conditioning is not to increase your oxygen uptake or VO2 max: anaerobic conditioning does that. Aerobic conditioning moves oxygen through the body allowing for an increase in the transportation of oxygen and nutrients to working muscles. Such activity assists in the changing of body composition and tissue repair. The latter of these more important to the pitcher as one of the goals of a pitcher is the process of repairing the body between starts, and from workouts. Aerobic conditioning can provide a benefit in terms of promoting oxygen and blood flow for tissue repair.

The type, frequency and amount of aerobic exercise one should incorporate into their training is very much dependent training variables and time of year. Off-season, in-season, and spring training will dictate the amount of aerobic conditioning performed. The duration and frequency of aerobic training can range from 2-4 days per week and session times of 20-45 minutes.

Many pitchers in the big leagues dependent upon their role may perform a small amount of aerobic training daily or a more extensive session the day after a start. This broad range allows for flexibility in incorporating aerobic training into your overall conditioning program.

Numerous choices such as running poles at a moderate pace, stationary biking, or even the treadmill in the weight room exist for your aerobic conditioning. The modality chosen to complete this section of your training is again determined by individual factors. Regardless of the choice in aerobic training modalities, it is very important to execute your aerobic conditioning at the correct intensity. A simple test I utilize to determine if you are working at a good intensity is the "talk test". During your aerobic training session, train at a level where you are working hard, but still able to have a normal conversation with someone standing next to you. Relative to your training program, it is ideal to place aerobic training sessions at the end of your program.

Anaerobic Conditioning

The modalities, execution of exercises, outcome and variables associated with anaerobic training are completely different than those of aerobic conditioning. The goal of anaerobic training is to improve the oxygen uptake capacities of your cardiovascular system (measured uniformly by your VO2 max). Let's take an example of anaerobic activity to better define and understand it.

Sprint work may be the easiest example of anaerobic training to understand. Sprinting a specified distance for a certain number of repetitions with a rest interval in between each sprint will increase over time the efficiency at which oxygen uptake occurs, thus improving your VO2 max and anaerobic capacities. Running poles is a prime example of a common anaerobic conditioning activity of the pitcher.

The benefits of anaerobic training are; an increase in the amount and rate of oxygen that is delivered to working muscles, a decrease in the rate at which muscular fatigue sets in during physical activity, a reduced recovery time and increases in speed. All of which are beneficial to the pitcher. That being said anaerobic conditioning is a very necessary part of a pitcher's conditioning program.

Relative to the pitcher there are a number of choices in terms of anaerobic training modalities. This again depends upon the time of the year (off-season, spring training, off-season) and what is available in terms of equipment and facilities. Jump rope intervals are a great off-season anaerobic training modality. A heavy or light rope can be used for this exercise and slight changes in effort levels should be made during the season relative to the off-season. Another beneficial anaerobic training modality for pitchers in the off-season is interval sprints on the bike. Simply use a stationary bike and create an interval time of maximum effort followed by a rest period. Spring training and during the season allow us usage of the field for our anaerobic training and this where we can implement programming such as poles discussed above or other sprint orientated activities. Regardless of the modality chosen to complete your anaerobic training, a time frame of 8-10 minutes should suffice for this section of your training. The frequency of anaerobic training is dictated by the time of year (in-season, off-season, pre-season). In-season anaerobic training should be performed 1-2 times per week, where as in the off-season up to 3 anaerobic training sessions per week is viable.

Nutrition

The food consumed on a daily basis and during a round of golf will affect how well you play. I utilize the phrase "food is fuel" when discussing nutrition relative to the athlete. Good nutrition equals good fuel for the body and results in you feeling better and playing better. On the flip side, poor nutrition equals bad fuel causing less than optimal play and poor health.

All too often nutrition is forgotten in the minds of the ball player and overlooked as it relates to health, wellness, improved physical conditioning, and recovery. That being said, pitchers of any age can improve their health, wellness and game with sound nutrition.

Nutrition can be very basic. Essentially what will affect your round. It is key when on the course to provide your body with proper hydration and fuel during the course of the game. It is best to hydrate with water or a sports drink during a game. A fuel source in the form of complex carbohydrates, good fats, and proteins will provide sustained energy from the first pitch to the last. Convenient food sources such as nuts, fruits, and certain nutritional bars are ideal for your round of golf.

To achieve a sensible diet grounded upon basic nutrition is quite easy. In the most basic of terms we have carbohydrates, fats, and proteins. I break each of these categories down into "good" and "bad". Eat good carbohydrates, fats and proteins you will do splendidly. Consume too many "bad" carbohydrates, fats and proteins problems will occur. Now let's take a look at each of these categories to allow you a better understanding on how what you eat impacts your performance.

Carbohydrates are the main fuel source for the body. Carbohydrates are broken down into sugar by your body and used for energy. Energy to walk, talk, drive a car, and throw a baseball. We need carbohydrates to function on a day-to-day basis. The key component as it relates to carbohydrates is the type ("good" or "bad"). Good carbohydrates consist of complex sugars that are burned slowly by the body, providing you long-term energy. Bad carbohydrates consist of simple sugars, which are burned very quickly, causing spikes in blood sugar, and bouts of low energy. Sources of good carbohydrates are apples, whole grain breads, beans, all-bran cereals, and whole oats. Bad carbohydrates are any foods containing large amounts of simple sugars such as candy bars, donuts, soda, and white bread. Basically, avoid foods with bad carbohydrates and eat the good ones.

Proteins are commonly referred to as "the building blocks of the body". The reason for this is proteins assist in the repair and building of new tissue. Any activity involving your muscles causes the breakdown of tissue within the body. In order to repair this tissue and build new tissue the body requires sources of protein. For example, golf fitness exercises require exertion from your muscles. This activity creates micro-tears in your muscles. In order to repair these micro-tears, protein is required.

Good proteins can be classified as lean cuts of beef, chicken, turkey, fish, eggs, tofu, and even nuts. Bad proteins contain a high level of saturated fats either naturally or from having been cooked in bad fats. For example, a lean cut of beef cooked in butter becomes a bad protein; not because of the protein source itself, but rather from it being cooked in butter. Stick with lean cuts of beef, skinless chicken, turkey, fish, and nuts for your protein sources. Avoid foods that are fried, and pay attention to how you cook it. Do note the body can use protein as an energy source but it is much better off with energy supplied from good fats and carbohydrates.

All too often fats are thought of as bad for your health. This is a misconception. Your body requires the consumption of some fats for day-to-day functioning. Just as carbohydrates and proteins can either be good or bad, fats can as well. Good fats can be found in food sources such as avocados, salmon, nuts, and olive oil. These fats sources provide your body with long-term energy sources as well as assisting in the transfer of nutrients at a cellular level. Bad fats, on the other hand, contain high levels of saturated fat and are not used efficiently by the body. Butter, bacon, fatty meats, fried chicken, French fries, potato chips, and many fast food items should be avoided. Basically, avoid bad fats and consume sources of good fats.

Results in your strength and conditioning program require sound nutrition. The body must be provided with good sources of fuel on and off the mound. This will allow for the gains you are attempting to make as a pitcher become a reality.

Improvement of your nutrition is a long-term project; there are no "quick fixes" as it pertains to healthy nutrition. I suggest thinking about nutrition as you do improving as a pitcher; it takes time, dedication, and commitment to the right food choices. Put a plan in place, be dedicated to that plan, and be patient. Dividends in your game will be the result.

Recovery

Aerobic conditioning, anaerobic conditioning, and nutrition have been the focal points of this chapter. A fourth component, recovery, requires attention as well. Recovery can be defined as the process of your body repairing and preparing itself for daily life, physical activity, training, and/or sport. Repairing is defined as the process of providing your body the proper rest/nutrition, preparing is the physical task of training/practice to perform your chosen sport. Recovery incorporates both the preparation and repairing process.

Recovery for pitchers is broken down into two segments. Segment number one is the recovery time between sets and exercises within your training program. Recovery time (i.e. rest periods) between sets/exercises drastically affects the physical outcome of your golf fitness training. For example, if you were in the power training section of your training program and resting only 30 seconds between each set of overhead medicine ball throws, this would be too little of a rest between each set of exercises for this type of training. The incorrect rest period in the above example would result in less gain from the exercise.

The table below breaks down the ideal rest periods between each segment of your training program. Table 1.7 will assist in determining the proper rest periods between each set of exercise in your strength and conditioning program.

Table 1.7 Recovery Time for Exercise Modalities

TYPE OF TRAINING	REPETITION/SETS	REST PERIODS	FREQUENCY WORKOUTS
Warm-up	5-15	Minimal	6
Flexibility	30-45 sec. Hold	Minimal	4-6
Balance	8-15	30 seconds	3-4
Pillar Strength	6-15	30 seconds	3-4
Functional Strength	5-12	60 seconds	3-4
Power	3-10	2 minutes	3-4

The above table clearly indicates how recovery time significantly affects the outcome of your training program. Utilize this table in accordance to the segment of your program to obtain the greatest benefit from your training.

The second segment of recovery encompasses the rest period between your workouts. Table 1.7, in addition to providing information on rest periods between sets, also offers information on the frequency of your training. For example, warm-up and flexibility training require little recovery time for your body. This allows you to implement these segments more frequently into your program, almost on a daily basis. Balance, torso strength, and functional strength exercises necessitate a larger recovery period between exercise bouts. A recovery time of anywhere between 24-36 hours is needed for these types of exercises. Power is on the other side of the spectrum relative to warm-up/flexibility exercises. This type of training requires 48-72 hours between sessions. These recovery periods allow your body to repair micro-trauma resulting from the workout. In addition, following these recovery guidelines between exercise sessions will prepare your body for the next training session.

It is very important to keep in mind recovery is an essential component of any training program. Too much training can result in less than optimal results from your program, and, in addition, can be counterproductive to your throwing program.

Summary

Advancement in your game not only requires improving as a pitcher and fitness components of the body, but also requires the inclusion of aerobic training, anaerobic training, sound nutrition, and proper recovery. The incorporation of these components into your comprehensive throwing program will provide you with the greatest amount of success from your efforts on and off the mound.

Chapter Thirteen

Strength & Conditioning Programs

We are now ready to put all this information into your own training program. Chapter 13 will present you with guidelines to design, implement, and alter your workout program to your own individual needs and schedule. While reading through this chapter keep in mind all the information you have previous learned. Refer back to previous chapters if necessary. This is the point where you design a training program to your specific needs and goals as a pitcher.

Before beginning your pitcher specific training program, you must determine that goals and needs of your training. For example, if you find that you are lacking the needed core strength to stabilize the body and arm fatigue in the latter innings. Then a specific portion should focus on the development of additional core and joint integrity strength/endurance. This chapter will begin by guiding you through the process of designing of your own training program. Pitcher specific training programs for beginners to advanced players will be reviewed, and an introduction of some advanced training techniques will be presented for your viewing. Individuals with a strong background in resistance training may utilize the more advanced training techniques immediately. Always remember to be cross specific with all of your training modalities.

Program Design

Every individual will have different goals, exercises, and variables within their pitcher specific training program. Due to this reason, the first step in any resistance training program is determining your personal needs. The second step is to develop a training program that meets those needs. These two parameters require you to start off with what is termed a "needs analysis". The second step within this process after an assessment is determining what your goals are within this training program. You must initially invest a little time on these two steps or you will find yourself putting in a great deal of time and effort into a training program, and getting marginal results!

Needs Analysis and Training Goals

A needs analysis essentially entails determining what requirements your pitcher specific training must meet. Two areas must be focused upon when preparing your needs analysis. Discussed many times throughout this book has been the idea of cross specificity: train specifically to the positions, movements, and athletic requirements of a pitcher. At this point you want to further delineate this concept to what you need as a pitcher. For example, a starter on a major league roster has definitively different requirements of their training program than does a closer or middle relief pitcher.

This will allow for a more specialized program to be developed. The second factor of information that needs to be attained from your "needs analysis" is individual areas that need improvement. For example, if you are lacking strength endurance in the lower extremities (i.e. legs/hips), then a key to a portion of your training needs to focus on developing this parameter in the legs and torso. Overall, your analysis process aims at developing a map of specific neuromuscular requirements that are needed by you as a pitcher. The analysis will also highlight the areas that require your attention to improve as an individual ball player.

The final step is mapping out your training goals. Once you have determined the "needs" of your position on the staff, and your "needs" as an individual, a list of training goals for your training program may be developed. The main goal of your training is to improve yourself as a pitcher, but as stated above there may areas that need additional attention. Listed below are the goals of a comprehensive pitcher specific training program.

Baseball Specific Training Program Goals

- *Develop required joint mobility*

- *Improve balance*

- *Improved stabilization*

- *Increase in core strength/endurance/power*

- *Improvement in neuromuscular flexibility parameters*

- *Neuromuscular endurance*

- *Development of neuromuscular strength endurance*

- *Increased neuromuscular strength*

- *Improved neuromuscular power outputs*

- *Increases in neuromuscular endurance*

- *Improve arm health*

- *Develop high levels of joint integrity strength and endurance*

You can see from the above list that a pitcher specific training program has many areas that it directs you in terms of developing your neuromuscular system. This brings us to the point of putting all the information in this book into a sequential order to follow during your day-to-day training.

Order of Pitcher Specific Training Program

An ideal pitcher specific training program follows a sequence. The recommended sequence to follow on a day-to-day basis, this allows for proper ratios of balance, stabilization, flexibility, core, joint stabilization, resistance training exercises, power, aerobic and anaerobic exercises to be performed.

Warm up, Flexibility, and Mobility Exercises

The dynamic warm up, flexibility, and mobility exercises is the first section of your programming and always should be. The foam roll, static flexibility, dynamic range of motion, and mobility exercises not only develop the required levels of flexibility and mobility in the kinetic chain but also prepare the body. This preparation is via activation and moving the body through multi-joing/multi-directional movement patterns.

Power Exercises

The next series of protocols in your individualized pitcher training program are power drills. Make sure before you begin any power training activities you have developed a foundation within your neuromuscular system. This foundation is a direct result of your balance, stabilization, core, and functional training. Allow at least 4 to 6 weeks of consisted training with the modalities listed above to allow for a base of "strength" in these parameters to have been developed. The goals of your power exercises are to develop speed and power within the neuromuscular system. At times with younger players this section of the program may be moved behind the joint integrity and pillar training sections of the training program. The reason behind such a shift is prioritization of training goals within the individual pitcher.

Balance, Stabilization, and Pillar Exercises

A very important segment of your training, if the capacities of balance, stabilization, and pillar strength/endurance are not developed the functional strength created in the neuromuscular system will be less than optimal because your body will not be able to maintain of body position/body control to utilize that strength. This is imperative to the pitcher and arm health. A "weak core" places greater stress on the arm and we can obviously see the concerns with such a situation.

These exercises focus on developing the parameters of balance and stabilization in the entire neuromuscular system. The torso strengthening exercises will develop strength and endurance in the core section of the body. If the torso section of the body is ignored then again the strength/power created in the lower extremities will be less than optimal because energy transferred through the kinetic chain will be limited by the weak musculature of the torso.

Joint Integrity

This section of exercises addresses the rotator cuff, scapular, and shoulder complex improving the strength and endurance capacities within these anatomical sections of the kinetic chain. We recognize the high incidence of arm injuries, the high levels of stress placed upon these structures, and the need to independently develop these areas of the body to withstand the repetitive movement trauma of the throwing motion.

Functional Exercise

At this point you are ready to start your functional strength training exercises. Remember, these exercises are cross specific to the positions, movements, and neuromuscular actions that you perform in this sport. The rational behind cross specificity training is the transfer of training effect. Training the neuromuscular system specific to the positions, movements, and actions results in a optimal performance on the mound. If your resistance training exercises are not cross specific then the results from your hard work will be less than optimal. As a result of the requirements of a pitcher, your functional resistance training protocols will incorporate multi-planar, multi-dimensional, endurance, strength endurance, power, speed, and balance exercises.

Up to this point we have reviewed the proper training sequence for a baseball specific conditioning program. The sequence is as follows: (1) dynamic warm up, flexibility, and mobility exercises, (2) power training, (3) balance/stabilization/core exercises, (4) joint integrity, and (5) functional resistance training exercises. This gives you an outline to follow when developing your individualized pitcher specific conditioning/training program. At this point, a series of sample conditioning programs will be presented fro beginners to advance. We will look at both an in-season and off-season program for each classification.

Periodization Schedules

Recalling chapter two, periodization is a process of cycling loads, volumes, intensity, and exercises within a given time period. The times frames can be divided into weeks, months and even years. Each time frame has a specific arrangement of load, volume, intensity, and exercises within the given time frame. The cycles of a periodization program are broken down into macrocycles and microcycles.

A macrocycle is the complete training time, which is usually one year. A mesocycle is a specific time frame within the macrocycle (for example, one baseball season). The mesocycle is usually planned around the differing portions of the year for the ball player (in-season, off-season, pre-season). The subdivisions of mesocycles for the baseball in a linear periodization schedule are as follows:

Phase 1: strength and endurance training. The body gains muscular strength and endurance.

Phase 2: strength training. The body continues strength development in the muscular system and power training is introduced. Training intensity increases and overall volume remains the same or decreases.

Phase 3: power training: The body develops increased power outputs. Training intensity increases and overall volume decreases.

Phase 4: sports-specific training: Sport-specific movements are refined, and the athlete focuses upon the upcoming season. Training intensity and volume decreases.

Phase 5: competition/maintenance training. Intensity is lower and volume decreased so that the athlete can on competition.

The pitcher will typically find phases 1, 2, and 3 in the off-season portion of their program, phase 4 in the pre-season (spring training), and phase 5 during the season. The phases within the periodization program allow for a systematic introduction of increased training intensities, volumes, and additional variables into the ball players training program. This allows the body to gradually adapt to new stresses placed upon it and peak correctly for key events during the season.

Utilizing a scheme popularized by strength and conditioning coach Janet Alexander, we can input the mesocycle phases listed above into "blocks" for the off-season, pre-season, and in-season phases of the mesocycle. Each block represents one 7-day training week. For example, block number one in the off-season represents the first week of training during the off-season training schedule. Block number two represents the second week of the off-season schedule and each consecutive block would correlate to the next week for the remainder of the off-season schedule. Using this system of blocks creates a very simple process in terms of developing a pitcher's off-season, pre-season and in-season periodization schedule. All that is required for the utilization of the block system is to determine the number of weeks each segment (off-season, pre-season, in-season) will contain within the year for the pitcher.

For example, a professional baseball player typically has an 10-12 week off-season training time after an active rest post-season, this portion of the periodization schedule would then contain ten to twelve blocks (one block for each week). Each block representing one week would have a specific training goal with corresponding training volumes, intensities and exercises to achieve this goal. The tendency for most athletes in the off-season would have blocks 1-4work on developing phase 1 of the mesocycle, blocks 5-8 build phase 2 of the mesocycle, and blocks 9-12 train phase 3 of the mesocycle.

I am a strong proponent of both periodization schedules and Janet Alexander's block system in the implementation of training for athletes. Such programs allow for a systematic, structured and measurable process to occur in the training of these young athletes. I personally utilize both perdiozation schedules and the block system and would recommend you do the same.

Beginner Strength & Conditioning Program

Up to this point in this chapter we have discussed the importance of a needs analysis, goal setting and periodization schedules. We will now begin to assimilate all this information into a series of sample strength and conditioning programs. It is important to note the programs listed below are simply sample programs and are to be used only as guidelines in the development of your own individualized training program. The first sample program listed is the beginner strength and conditioning program.

The beginner program is ideal for the individual new to resistance training. I personally find it best to start all junior level players with a beginner lever program for the shear fact many of the exercises and training modalities are new for the athlete regardless of training experience. After the commencement of a beginner level program plan to spend 8 to 12 weeks at this level before moving onto the next. A time frame of 8 to 12 weeks will allow for your body to adapt to the new exercises, provide time for improvement in key areas for golf, and mastery of this program.

For the benefits of this program to become a reality it is imperative that you are consistent with your training. If you are consistent with your training, physical benefits and improvement should begin to be seen within 4-6 weeks.

It is strongly suggested you follow the program sequence listed in the first section of this chapter. Begin with a warm-up, move onto your flexibility exercises, proceed to your balance training and complete the program with the torso strength and functional exercises. This will provide your body the proper ratios of each type of training for improvement in your game. Power training is not a component of the beginner program because this type of training requires a base of flexibility, balance, strength, and endurance to perform correctly. This program will develop the foundation required for power training.

Guidelines:

3 times per week   1-2 sets per exercise   8-15 repetitions per set

Functional Warm-up Exercises:	**Sets:**	**Repetitions:**
Calf Foam Roll	1	5
Glute Foam Roll	1	5
IT Band Foam Roll	1	5
Quadriceps Foam Roll	1	5
Thoracic Foam Roll	1	5
Lat Foam Roll	1	5

Flexibility Exercises:	Sets:	Repetitions
90/90 Hamstring Stretch	1	30 second hold
Piriformis Stretch	1	30 second hold
Glute Stretch	1	30 second hold
Kneeling Hip Flexor	1	30 second hold
Quadriceps Stretch w/ Physio-Ball	1	30 second hold
Side Lunge Stretch	1	30 second hold
Lat Stretch w/ Physio– Ball	1	30 second hold

Functional Warm-up Exercises cont:	Sets:	Repetitions
Bent Knee Side-to-Side Leg Swings	1	10
Straight Leg Swings Side-to-Side	1	10
Straight Leg Swings Forward-Back	1	10
Bent Knee Tennis Ball Lifts	1	10
Flat Bench Hip Extensions	1	10
Forward Lunge w/ Reach	1	5
Side Lunge w/ Reach	1	5
Spider	1	5

Balance Exercises:	Sets:	Repetitions:
Single Leg Cone Reach	1	8
Single Leg Toe Touch	1	8

Pillar Strength Exercises:	Sets:	Repetitions:
Bent Knee Back Hold	1	30 second hold
Prone Hold	1	30 second hold
Side Hold	1	30 second hold
Alternating Arm and Leg Extension	1	10
Kneeling Cable Chops	1	10
Kneeling Cable Lifts	1	10
Side Leg Raise – Abduction	1	10
Side Leg Raise– Adduction	1	10

Joint Integrity Exercises:	Sets:	Repetitions:
Fore Arm Pinch Push Up	1	10
Kneeling Y-T-W-L	1	10

Functional Exercises:	Sets:	Repetitions:
Body Weight Squats	1	10
Bulgarian Split Squat	1	10
Good Mornings	1	10
Bent Knee Hip Extension	1	10
Tubing Press	1	10
Horizontal Pull Up	1	10

Intermediate Strength & Conditioning Program

The intermediate program is the next program as you advance. It will introduce power training into the program. At this time the athlete should be ready for the implementation of such exercises. Advancement from the beginner level to the intermediate level will occur within 8-12 weeks assuming you were consistent with your training.

The exercises found in the intermediate program will be more challenging, and the program will continue the progress seen in your swing from the beginner level program. In addition to the exercises becoming more challenging, the option to increase the frequency of your training from 3 days per week to 4 exists.

Always keep in mind with the intermediate program, in addition to the other sample programs found in this book, the uniqueness of every athlete. Each and every athlete has different needs and goals as it relates to training. As a result there is no one program that is the correct training program for every individual pitcher. The sample programs found in this book must be individualized to one's own requirements. Keep this point in mind and individualize each program to suit your own needs and goals.

Listed below are two sample intermediate level programs. Refer back to previous chapters for specific descriptions of each exercise. Execute each exercise with correct technique for the number of repetitions suggested. Do not compromise the form of each exercise to achieve a specific number of repetitions: rather perform the number of repetitions for the given exercise you can complete correctly.

Intermediate Strength & Conditioning Program One

Guidelines:

3 times per week   1-2 sets per exercise   5-15 repetitions per set

Functional Warm-up Exercises:	Sets:	Repetitions:
Calf Foam Roll	1	5
Glute Foam Roll	1	5
IT Band Foam Roll	1	5
Quadriceps Foam Roll	1	5
Thoracic Foam Roll	1	5
Lat Foam Roll	1	5

Flexibility Exercises:	Sets:	Repetitions
90/90 Hamstring Stretch	1	30 second hold
Piriformis Stretch	1	30 second hold
Glute Stretch	1	30 second hold
Kneeling Hip Flexor	1	30 second hold
Cat In-the –Wheel	1	30 second hold
Quadriceps Stretch w/ Physio-Ball	1	30 second hold
Side Lunge Stretch	1	30 second hold
Lat Stretch w/ Physio– Ball	1	30 second hold
Physio-Ball Chest Stretch	1	30 seconds hold

Functional Warm-up Exercises cont:	Sets:	Repetitions
Bent Knee Side-to-Side Leg Swings	1	10
Straight Leg Swings Side-to-Side	1	10
Straight Leg Swings Forward-Back	1	10
Bent Knee Tennis Ball Lifts	1	10
Flat Bench Hip Extensions	1	10
Forward Lunge w/ Reach	1	10
Side Lung w/ Reach	1	10
Spider	1	10

Power Exercises:	Sets:	Repetitions:
Kneeling Medicine Ball Side Throw	2	6
Box Jump	2	6

Balance Exercises:	Sets:	Repetitions:
Balance Pad Single Leg Cone Reach	1	10
Balance Pad Single Leg Toe Touch	1	10
Single Leg Airplane Rotations	1	10

Pillar Strength Exercises:	Sets	Repetitions
Physio-Ball Roll Outs	1	15
Physio-Ball Straight Arm Side-to-Side	1	15
Physio-Ball Table Top	1	15
Physio-Ball Jack Knife	1	15
Physio-Ball Russian Twist	1	15

Tubing Walks	1	10

Joint Integrity Exercises:	Sets:	Repetitions:
Fore Arm Pinch Push Ups	1	15
Tubing Adduction	1	10
Tubing Internal-External Rotation	1	10
Tubing External Rotation at 90	1	10
Kneeling Y-T-W-L	1	10

Functional Exercises:	Sets:	Repetitions:
Weighted Vest Bulgarian Split Squat	2	8
Suite Case Dead Lift	2	8
Physio-Ball Chest Press	2	8
Pull Up	2	8
Single Arm Dumbbell Row	2	8

Anaerobic Conditioning:

60-yard Sprint Intervals (60 yard sprint, 30 seconds rest) x 4

Intermediate Strength & Conditioning Program Two

Guidelines:

4 times per week	Alternate between Program A and B	1-3 sets per exercise	5-20 repetitions per set

Program A

Functional Warm-up Exercises:	Sets:	Repetitions:
Calf Foam Roll	1	5
Glute Foam Roll	1	5
IT Band Foam Roll	1	5
Adductors Foam Roll	1	5
Thoracic Foam Roll	1	5
Lat Foam Roll	1	5

Flexibility Exercises:	Sets:	Repetitions
90/90 Hamstring Stretch	1	30 second hold
Piriformis Stretch	1	30 second hold
Glute Stretch	1	30 second hold
Kneeling Hip Flexor	1	30 second hold

Quadriceps Stretch w/ Physio-Ball	1	30 second hold
Side Lunge Stretch	1	30 second hold
Lat Stretch w/ Physio– Ball	1	30 second hold
Physio-Ball Chest Stretch	1	30 seconds hold

Functional Warm-up Exercises cont:	Sets:	Repetitions
Bent Knee Side-to-Side Leg Swings	1	10
Straight Leg Swings Side-to-Side	1	10
Straight Leg Swings Forward-Back	1	10
Bent Knee Tennis Ball Lifts	1	10
Flat Bench Hip Extensions	1	10
Forward Lunge w/ Reach	1	10
Side Lung w/ Reach	1	10
Spider	1	10

Balance Exercises:	Sets:	Repetitions:
Single Leg Airplane Rotations	1	10

Power Exercises:	Sets:	Repetitions:
Kneeling Medicine Ball Side Throw	2	8
Kneeling Overhead Med Ball Throw	2	8

Pillar Strength Exercises:	Sets:	Repetitions:
Physio-Ball Roll Outs	2	15
Physio-Ball Straight Arm Side-to-Side	2	15
Physio-Ball Jack Knife	2	15
Physio-Ball Russian Twist	2	15
Tubing Walks	1	15

Joint Integrity Exercises:	Sets:	Repetitions:
Fore Arm Pinch Push Up	1	10
Tubing Adduction	1	10
Tubing Internal-External Rotation	1	10
Tubing External Rotation at 90	1	10

Functional Exercises:	Sets:	Repetitions:
Jefferson Squat	2	8
Weighted Vest Bulgarian Split Squat	2	8
Weighted Vest Step Up	2	8
Pull Up	2	8
Single Arm Lat Pull Down	2	8
Single Arm Dumbbell Row	2	8

Program B

Functional Warm-up Exercises:	Sets:	Repetitions:
Calf Foam Roll	1	5
Glute Foam Roll	1	5
IT Band Foam Roll	1	5
Adductors Foam Roll	1	5
Thoracic Foam Roll	1	5
Lat Foam Roll	1	5

Flexibility Exercises:	Sets:	Repetitions
90/90 Hamstring Stretch	1	30 second hold
Piriformis Stretch	1	30 second hold
Glute Stretch	1	30 second hold
Kneeling Hip Flexor	1	30 second hold
Quadriceps Stretch w/ Physio-Ball	1	30 second hold
Side Lunge Stretch	1	30 second hold
Lat Stretch w/ Physio– Ball	1	30 second hold
Physio-Ball Chest Stretch	1	30 seconds hold

Functional Warm-up Exercises cont:	Sets:	Repetitions
Bent Knee Side-to-Side Leg Swings	1	10
Straight Leg Swings Side-to-Side	1	10
Straight Leg Swings Forward-Back	1	10
Bent Knee Tennis Ball Lifts	1	10
Flat Bench Hip Extensions	1	10
Forward Lunge w/ Reach	1	10
Side Lung w/ Reach	1	10

Spider	1	10

Power Exercises:	Sets:	Repetitions:
Scoop Throw	2	8
Box Jump	2	8

Balance Exercises:	Sets:	Repetitions:
Balance Pad Single Leg Cone Reach	1	10
Balance Pad Single Leg Toe Touch	1	10

Joint Integrity Exercises:	Sets:	Repetitions:
Kneeling Y-T-W-L	1	10
Overhead Medicine Ball Throws	1	50
Medicine Ball Wall Throws Left/Right	1	25

Pillar Strength Exercises:	Sets:	Repetitions:
Physio-Ball Table Top	2	15
Cable Press Outs	2	15
Physio-Ball Back Press	2	15

Functional Exercises:	Sets:	Repetitions:
Barbell Dead Lift	2	8
Single Leg Dumbbell Dead Lift	2	8
Kneeling Lunge Dumbbell Overhead Press	2	8

Advanced Strength & Conditioning Program

Once you have trained at the intermediate level program for 8 to 12 weeks, it is time to move onto the advanced level program. The intensity level will again increase at this level. Two advanced level training programs are delineated below. Again, it is recommended to adjust the sample programs to meet your own individual needs. Refer back to previous chapters for detailed exercise descriptions, pay strict attention to technique and perform the exercises to the best of your ability.

Advanced Strength & Conditioning Program One

Guidelines:

3 times per week	1-2 sets per exercise	5-15 repetitions per set

Functional Warm-up Exercises:	Sets:	Repetitions:
Calf Foam Roll	1	5
Glute Foam Roll	1	5
IT Band Foam Roll	1	5
Adductors Foam Roll	1	5
Thoracic Foam Roll	1	5
Lat Foam Roll	1	5

Flexibility Exercises:	Sets:	Repetitions
90/90 Hamstring Stretch	1	30 second hold
Piriformis Stretch	1	30 second hold
Glute Stretch	1	30 second hold
Kneeling Hip Flexor	1	30 second hold
Quadriceps Stretch w/ Physio-Ball	1	30 second hold
Side Lunge Stretch	1	30 second hold
Lat Stretch w/ Physio– Ball	1	30 second hold
Physio-Ball Chest Stretch	1	30 seconds hold

Functional Warm-up Exercises cont:	Sets:	Repetitions
Bent Knee Side-to-Side Leg Swings	1	10
Straight Leg Swings Side-to-Side	1	10
Straight Leg Swings Forward-Back	1	10
Bent Knee Tennis Ball Lifts	1	10
Flat Bench Hip Extensions	1	10
Forward Lunge w/ Reach	1	10
Side Lung w/ Reach	1	10
Spider	1	10

Power Exercises:	Sets:	Repetitions:
Side Throw Long Response	2	8
Overhead Scoop Throw	2	8
Multiple Hurdle Jumps	2	8

Balance Exercises:	Sets:	Repetitions:
Balance Pad Single Leg Cone Reach	1	10

	Sets:	Repetitions:
Balance Pad Single Leg Toe Touch	1	10
Side-to-Side Stabilization Hops	1	8

Pillar Strength Exercises:	Sets:	Repetitions:
Physio-Ball Forearm Saws	2	15
Physio-Ball Straight Arm Side-to-Side	2	15
Cable Press Outs	2	15
Physio-Ball Russian Twist	2	15
Tubing Walks	1	15

Joint Integrity Exercises:	Sets:	Repetitions:
Fore Arm Pinch Push Ups	1	15
Tubing Adduction	1	15
Tubing Internal-External Rotation	1	15
Tubing External Rotation at 90	1	15
Kneeling Y-T-W-L	1	15

Functional Exercises:	Sets:	Repetitions:
Goblet Squat	3	8
Single Leg Dumbbell Dead Lift	3	8
Physio-Ball Dumbbell Chest Press	3	8
Pull Up	3	8
Single Arm Dumbbell Row	3	8

Anaerobic Conditioning:

60-yard Sprint Intervals (60 yard sprint, 20 seconds rest) x 6

Advanced Strength & Conditioning Program Two

Guidelines:

4 times per week   Alternate between Program A and B   1-3 sets per exercise   5-20 repetitions per set

Program A

Functional Warm-up Exercises:	Sets:	Repetitions:
Calf Foam Roll	1	5
Glute Foam Roll	1	5
IT Band Foam Roll	1	5

Adductors Foam Roll	1	5
Thoracic Foam Roll	1	5
Lat Foam Roll	1	5

Flexibility Exercises:	**Sets:**	**Repetitions**
90/90 Hamstring Stretch	1	30 second hold
Piriformis Stretch	1	30 second hold
Glute Stretch	1	30 second hold
Kneeling Hip Flexor	1	30 second hold
Quadriceps Stretch w/ Physio-Ball	1	30 second hold
Side Lunge Stretch	1	30 second hold
Lat Stretch w/ Physio– Ball	1	30 second hold
Physio-Ball Chest Stretch	1	30 seconds hold

Functional Warm-up Exercises cont:	**Sets:**	**Repetitions**
Bent Knee Side-to-Side Leg Swings	1	10
Straight Leg Swings Side-to-Side	1	10
Straight Leg Swings Forward-Back	1	10
Bent Knee Tennis Ball Lifts	1	10
Flat Bench Hip Extensions	1	10
Forward Lunge w/ Reach	1	10
Side Lunge w/ Reach	1	10
Spider	1	10

Power Exercises:	**Sets:**	**Repetitions:**
Overhead Scoop Throw	2	8
Multiple Hurdle Jumps	2	8

Balance Exercises:	**Sets:**	**Repetitions:**
Balance Pad Single Leg Airplane Rotations	1	15
Single Leg Box Hops	1	10

Pillar Strength Exercises:	**Sets:**	**Repetitions:**
Physio-Ball Forearm Saws	2	15
Physio-Ball Straight Arm Side-to-Side	2	15

Physio-Ball Jack Knife	2	15
Physio-Ball Russian Twist	2	15
Tubing Walks	1	15

Joint Integrity Exercises:	Sets:	Repetitions:
Fore Arm Pinch Push Ups	1	15
Tubing Adduction	1	15
Tubing Internal-External Rotation	1	15
Tubing External Rotation at 90	1	15

Functional Exercises:	Sets:	Repetitions:
Dumbbell Goblet Squat	3	8
Dumbbell Step Up	3	8
Pull Up	3	8
Single Arm Dumbbell Row	3	8

Anaerobic Conditioning:

60-yard Sprint Intervals (60 yard sprint, 20 seconds rest) x 6

Program B

Functional Warm-up Exercises:	Sets:	Repetitions:
Calf Foam Roll	1	5
Glute Foam Roll	1	5
IT Band Foam Roll	1	5
Adductors Foam Roll	1	5
Thoracic Foam Roll	1	5
Lat Foam Roll	1	5

Flexibility Exercises:	Sets:	Repetitions
90/90 Hamstring Stretch	1	30 second hold
Piriformis Stretch	1	30 second hold
Glute Stretch	1	30 second hold
Kneeling Hip Flexor	1	30 second hold
Quadriceps Stretch w/ Physio-Ball	1	30 second hold
Side Lunge Stretch	1	30 second hold
Lat Stretch w/ Physio– Ball	1	30 second hold

Physio-Ball Chest Stretch	1	30 seconds hold

Functional Warm-up Exercises cont:	**Sets:**	**Repetitions**
Bent Knee Side-to-Side Leg Swings	1	10
Straight Leg Swings Side-to-Side	1	10
Straight Leg Swings Forward-Back	1	10
Bent Knee Tennis Ball Lifts	1	10
Flat Bench Hip Extensions	1	10
Forward Lunge w/ Reach	1	10
Side Lung w/ Reach	1	10
Spider	1	10

Power Exercises:	**Sets:**	**Repetitions:**
Overhead Scoop Throw	2	8
Multiple Hurdle Jumps	2	8

Balance Exercises:	**Sets:**	**Repetitions:**
Balance Pad Single Leg Airplane Rotations	1	10
Single Leg Box Jumps	1	10

Pillar Strength Exercises:	**Sets:**	**Repetitions:**
Physio-Ball Table Tops	2	15
Physio-Ball Jack Knife	2	15
Physio-Ball Back Press	2	15

Joint Integrity Exercises:	**Sets:**	**Repetitions:**
Kneeling Y-T-W-L	1	15
Medicine Ball Overhead Throws	1	75
Medicine Ball Wall Throws Left/Right	1	50

Functional Exercises:	**Sets:**	**Repetitions:**
Barbell Dead Lift	3	8
Single Leg Dumbbell Dead Lift	3	8
Kneeling Dumbbell Shoulder Press	3	8

Summary

The final chapter of this book has provided you a comprehensive set of strength and conditioning programs. I suggest using these programs as samples for the development of your own individualized training program. Proceed at your own pace through the programs and use the time frames as guidelines only. A periodization schedule is integral in the development of a pitcher and should be followed.

Use all the information in this book to your benefit. Understand the importance of mobility, stability and power as it relates to pitching. Educate yourself on the training principles to adhere to as a baseball player. Most of all enjoy the process of improving as a pitcher. Thank you for giving me the opportunity to assist you in this process.

About the Author

Sean Cochran is the Founder and Director of Sean Cochran Sports Peformance and one of the most recognized performance coaches in sport today. Sean began his career in professional athletics in 1999 as a strength and conditioning coach of the Milwaukee Brewers of Major League Baseball. Cochran transitioned from the Brewers to his adopted hometown of San Diego in 2000 where he accepted the position of Strength and Conditioning Coordinator for the San Diego Padres. During his tenure in Major League Baseball, Sean had the opportunity to train World Series MVP Cole Hamels, Cy Young Award Winners Barry Zito and Jake Peavy, and second in all time saves leader Trevor Hoffman.

Sean was introduced to professional golf on the PGA Tour in late 2003. Since his introduction to golf Cochran has had the opportunity to work with numerous PGA Tour and LPGA players most notably 3-time Masters, PGA, and British Open Champion Phil Mickelson. In addition to Mickelson, Sean has worked with U.S. Open Champion Corey Pavin, PGA Tour and Senior U.S. Open Champion Peter Jacobsen, Ryder Cup Member and PGA Tour Winner Brad Faxon, PGA Championship Winner Shaun Michel, and LPGA Winners Hee Won Han, IK Kim, and Jennifer Johnson.

In addition to his work in professional athletics, Sean has authored and produced over 10 publications and numerous training videos related to sports performance training, has been a contributing author to PGATOUR.com, has served as a corporate ambassador to fortune 500 companies, product endorsee, and presenter at numerous educational seminars. Since the grand opening of Sean Cochran Sports Performance Training Facility, Sean has had the opportunity to train athletes in multiple sports including football, baseball, and golf with a focus on mentoring high school athletes.

Sean's accreditations include National Strength and Conditioning Association (1997), United States Weightlifting Federation (1998), American Sports Medicine Institute (1996), and the National Academy of Sports Medicine (2001, 2004).

COCHRAN'S STATS

- 8 Professional Golf Major Championships
- 2 CY Young Award Winners
- 7 MLB All Stars
- 4 Ryder Cup Team Members
- 5 President's Cup Team Members
- 8 first round MLB Draft Choices
- Multiple PGA Tour & LPGA Tour Winners
- Numerous MLB Draft Choices
- Multiple Division I Athletic Scholarship Recipients

Bibliography

Baechle, T.R., R.W. Earle, and D. Wathen. 2000 Resistance Training. In *Essentials of Strength Training and Conditioning* (2nd ed.), edited by T.R. Baechle and R.W. Earle. Champaign, IL: Human Kinetics

Boyle, M. 2004 Plyometric Training for Power, Targeted Torso Training and Rotational Strength. In *Functional Training for Sports*, edited by E. McNeely. Champaign, IL: Human Kinetics

Clark, M. 2001 Integrated Training, Human Movement Science, Current Concepts in Flexibility Training, Core Stabilization Training, Neuromuscular Stabilization Training. In *Integrated Training for the New Millennium*, edited by J. Jackson. Thousand Oaks, CA: National Academy of Sports Medicine

Cook, G. 2003 Mobility and Stability. In *Athletic Body in Balance*, edited by M. Barnard. Champaign, IL: Human Kinetics

Enoka, R. 1998 Human Movement Forces, Torque, Musckoskeletal Organization, Movement Strategies. In *Neuromechanical Basis of Kinesiology*, edited by R. Frey. Champaign, IL: Human Kinetics

Houglum, P. 2013 *An Analysis of the biomechanics of pitching in baseball,* Champaign, IL: Human Kinetics

House, T. 1994 Throwing the Ball: Deception, Energy Translation, Launch, and Deceleration. In *The Pitching Edge*, Champaign, IL: Human Kinetics

House, T. 1996 Rehabilitative Training. In *Fit to Hit,* Champaign, IL: Human Kinetics

Murphy, Forney. 1997 Benefits of Complete Conditioning for the Baseball Player. In *Complete Conditioning for Baseball*, Champaign, IL: Human Kinetics

Nicholls, R. L. 2006, "Numerical Analysis of maximal bat performance in baseball". *Journal of Biomechanics*

Reyes, Francis, October 2009, "Acute Effects of Various Weighted Bat Warm-Up Protocols on Bat Velocity". *Journal of Strength and Conditioning Research*

Santanna, J.C. 2004, Training Variables in *The Essence of Program Design*, Boca Rotan, FL: Optimum Performance Systems

Verstegen, M. Williams P., 2004 Movement Prep, Prehab, Elasticity in *Core Performance*, edited by J. Williams. United States of America: Rodale

Welch, C.M.; S.A. Banks, F.F. Dook, P. Draovitcg. 1995, "Hitting a Baseball: A Biomechanical Description". *Journal of Orthopaedic and Sport Physical Therapy*

Made in the USA
Lexington, KY
29 April 2018